MAKE MORE MONEY SELLING YOUR HOME

MAKE MORE MONEY
SELLING YOUR HOME

by David Orange
B Sc (Est Man) FRICS FSVA

foulsham
LONDON·NEW YORK·TORONTO·SYDNEY

foulsham
Yeovil Road, Slough, Berkshire, SL1 4JH

ISBN 0–572–02004–X

Printed in GreatBritain
at St. Edmundsbury Press, Ltd;
Bury St. Edmunds, Suffolk.

ABOUT THE AUTHOR

David Orange, B Sc (Est Man) FRICS FSVA, is well qualified to write this book.

David became a partner in a top Midlands firm of estate agents at the age of 25. Within five years he was its managing director and owner of the eight office company. At the peak of the property boom in 1988, he took the opportunity to sell the business to a well known insurance company. He went on to become one of the highest paid estate agency executives in the country.

David has designed and lectured on numerous estate agency training courses. He has sold hundreds of houses through negotiation and seen many people both make and save substantial sums of money in selling their homes.

He has intimate knowledge of the ins and outs of refurbishing houses while his experience as a chartered surveyor (FRICS) has given him outstanding knowledge of the effect improvements have on the value of domestic properties.

ACKNOWLEDGEMENTS

Very special thanks once again to my long time friend Steven Morewood BA (Hons) Humanities, Ph.D.
I would also like to thank the Law Society for their permission to reproduce the forms contained in Appendix 3.

This book is dedicated to Beverley, Simon, Caroline and Jessica Rixon

CONTENTS

INTRODUCTION

Many people will move home several times in their lifetime – indeed, Britain leads the world in this area. During Margaret Thatcher's long reign as Prime Minister the owner-occupancy rate rose from 55.3 per cent in 1979 to 67 per cent in 1990 and looks set to climb even further.

Selling property does not come cheap and in some instances can bring on many financial headaches. Let's say, for example, that you sell your house for £80,000, then decide to purchase a larger property for £100,000. You'll probably end up with a bigger mortgage than before, but you have a more valuable property to show for it.

However, where you can save, or lose, considerable amounts of money is in the methods you choose to sell. The wrong moves in this vital area can land you with estate agents fees in excess of £2,000 and legal fees on the sale and purchase of over £2,500!

Timing your move into the market is also crucial if you are to maximise your profits and minimise the costs of moving elsewhere. It will be emphasised in this book again and again that you should consider your house as an investment. As such it can both escalate and decline in value according to the state of the market.

Generally speaking, a homeowner who chose to sell during the Thatcher years did extremely well, with house prices rising by as much as 250 per cent in some instances!

A home bought for £15,040 in the East Midlands in 1979 was fetching £53,128 a decade later. In London, which has the most expensive housing in Britain, average prices rose from £24,830 to £79,304 over the same period.

On the other hand the Thatcher era ended with the housing market depressed and prices falling. By the early 1990's some homeowners who had bought property within the price range £150,000 to £200,000 were facing the fact that their homes had fallen in value by 30 per cent. Many were unable to sell in a depressed market and were burdened by expensive mortgages.

SAVE MONEY SELLING YOUR HOME

You can save money selling your home:

1. By negotiating on the estate agent's fees. Examples are given later. You could stand to save several hundred pounds.

2. By keeping on legal fees as low as possible. In many cases you will avoid spending considerable sums not by direct negotiating but simply by ringing around! Remember that solicitors' time is expensive, so the more you can help your solicitor to save time the lower is his bill. For your reference, Appendix 3 contains specimens of the Law Society forms which you and your solicitor will need to complete before you can sell your property. Gather as much of the information they ask for as you can *before* sitting down with your solicitor.

3. By selling your own home *providing* you still get the maximum price possible.

4. By understanding the house market you are selling in and by being able to negotiate from a position of strength and not conceding anything unnecessarily.

5. By understanding that once your home is sold you are in the strongest position to save money in buying your next residence.

MAKE MONEY SELLING YOUR HOME

Among the most significant ways are:

1. By buying wisely in the first place.

2. By improving or renovating an older property and selling it at a profit.

3. Through presenting your home in the best possible way.

4. By judging the housing market and knowing the best time of year to sell and exposing your home to the widest market.

5. Through knowing how to negotiate with your prospective buyer to maximise your price.

6. By understanding what type of improvements will add value to your home and avoiding those which won't.

SECTION 1
SELLING YOUR HOME:
AN OVERVIEW

GENERAL CONSIDERATIONS

HOW DO YOU SELL YOUR HOME?

If you have had previous experience of selling a property you will already know some of the answers to this question – but obviously looking to avoid unnecessary costs this time around. Others may not have gone through the selling process before. Either way this book will prove invaluable to you.

The type of questions which a first time seller finds it easier to pose than answer are: – What is the legal process involved in selling? How should the house best be presented to maximise the price and therefore the profit? How do you go forward once someone is interested in buying your property? And last, but not least, who is best placed to sell the property?

The Main Steps To Follow When Selling Your Home

1. Decide that you are going to sell.

2. Finish off any necessary work and sorting out to ensure your home is best presented to sell it.

3. Have several free valuations from estate agents.

4. Decide by what means and who is going to sell your home.

5. Notify your solicitor.

6. Place your home on the market.

7. Show prospective viewers around and negotiate a price.

8. Notify solicitors. At this stage if you are also

buying a house you can firm up on any negotiations.

9. Plan the move.

10. Complete the transaction!

If you are buying a house as well I would refer you to the companion to this book *Save Money Buying Your Home*.

REASONS FOR SELLING YOUR HOME

It is first worth considering the reasons you may have to sell your house. Broadly, these fall into two categories: urgent and non-urgent. If you have to move quickly, for whatever reason, then you will have to make the best of the market conditions available. On the other hand, as you will see later in the book, if you are able to time your entry into the property market then, potentially, you can make and save more money.

So, let's look first at the more pressing reasons why you may feel compelled to move.

1. You have taken a new job outside the area. An estimated one in six people move for this reason.

2. Death, divorce or emigration. It is estimated that some 300,000 or so houses in the UK change

hands for these reasons every year.

3. You can no longer afford your mortgage and have to seek either a smaller property to reduce your financial obligations, rented accommodation or accommodation with family/friends until your circumstances improve.

Less vital reasons for selling your property will generally fall into the following categories.

1. Your present home is no longer large enough for your needs and you require somewhere bigger (and vice-versa). Clearly here a move is desirable as soon as possible but, unlike the preceding reasons, some flexibility over timing is still possible.

2. You realise that your house is the biggest investment you will ever make and the sooner you move up market the better. This reason is given by most people for wanting to move. At the same time, you can still decide *when* to sell.

3. You wish to cash in on your investment. Here the property may not be your own, but has been inherited, perhaps through the death of close relations. In 1980 bricks and mortar made up £2.16 billion of the inheritances received in Britain; by the end of the century it is estimated that this figure will have leaped to £28.79 billion.

WHAT PEOPLE ARE LOOKING FOR WHEN THEY SELL THEIR HOME

Whatever the reasons for selling, you must have clearly defined goals that you want to achieve from a sale. There are four main ones and these will form the core themes of this book. They are:

- the best possible price

- a speedy rather than a protracted sale

- the least hassle

- the need to keep the cost of selling as low as possible.

You will need to be flexible and to match up different goals one against the other. For example, normally you will be buying another property at the same time as you are selling your existing residence. Let's say that the property you wish to buy is made available for some £5,000 less than the price you would be willing to pay. It is evident you need to sell your property or the move may fall through. In this situation you can knock down the price of your home by several thousands of pounds to encourage a sale. Here, if you slashed £5,000 off the price you would be no worse off.

The moral is that the most important consideration is the difference between the selling and buying prices.

The quickest possible sale may not be your goal if you are in no rush to sell. There are plenty of people in this position who take their properties off the market to wait for a better selling climate, or because they have been frustrated in their search for a suitable new house.

SELLING A FLAT

Much of what will be said about selling a house also applies to selling a flat. There are, nonetheless, one or two points which need to be made if a flat rather than a house is involved.

The market is more limited. Not everybody wants to live in a flat. They are more attractive to single people than to families – especially large ones – where the more cramped conditions are an obvious drawback.

It may cost more in legal fees to sell a flat rather than a house. This is because in England and Wales most flats are sold lease-

hold and the legal toings and froings can be more involved.

If there is less than around 45 years to run on a lease many lenders will not permit a mortgage to be taken out on such a flat. Generally, building societies are not disposed to lend money on any lease below 70 years. For many of them the lease must be twice as long as the repayment period as security for their investment. This also can limit the number of potential buyers in the flat market.

WHEN TO SELL

Many people are convinced that the spring is the best time of the year to sell property. Whilst in many cases this may well be true, my advice would be that any time during the first half of a year is ideal. In this six month spell the maximum number of buyers, and especially first-time buyers, are out in force. Placing your home on the market at this time will therefore tend to generate more interest than at other times of the year.

Early January can sometimes be a busy time for house sales. This is not always so, however, because of the obvious spanner in the works represented by the weather. Heavy snow might well rule out a boom at this time while an extremely mild winter may create the conditions for hectic sales in the housing market as well as in the shops.

The worst times to try to sell are in November and December with Christmas looming, and July and August when holidays are at their most popular.

It should be pointed out that if you are buying as well as selling then the best time to sell is often the worst time to buy and vice-versa. But the important point to bear in mind is that it is the *difference between what you sell and buy for* which is the all important consideration.

THE HOUSING MARKET

The housing market is very cyclical with frequent ups and downs. Periods of rapidly increasing house prices such as 1973–4, 1978 and 1988 can be followed by very slow activity and even falling property prices. At other times prices may be static for long periods.

It's not difficult to find out what's happening to the housing market generally. Television, radio and newspapers will all be useful sources of information. Whether there's a housing boom or slump you need to know what happens in the marketplace.

When prices are rising steeply and there are more buyers than sellers we have what is called a "sellers' market". Here the seller of the house is able to call the tune to a great extent. The practice of "gazumping" – accepting a figure from one party but then accepting an increased bid from another – is a symptom of such a market. In a sellers' market you, as the property seller, are placed in a strong position in matters like price negotiation and making sure that the timing is convenient to you. There shouldn't be any shortage of offers, especially if your home is in a sought after location.

In a buyers' market, where house sales are generally static and prices are level or falling, the opposite is true. Many more properties will be available for sale than in a sellers' market. This state of affairs gives the buyer the upper hand. Knowing that the market is saturated with properties for sale, he can afford to pass up several opportunities. Bargain buys are the norm rather than the exception – but in the end your acceptance of any bid depends on how desperately you want to sell your house.

The housing market is also very regional in nature, with activity levels and price trends varying from one part of the country to another. Watch your local press for details of what is happening in your locality. For an overall view, several leading building societies can offer very useful house bulletins which will allow you to compare prices across the country. These are especially useful if you are thinking of moving out of your current area.

My own personal conviction is that while domestic property prices will rise in the 1990's they will do so less spectacularly than they did during the previous ten years. Governments now recognise the link between inflation and house prices – rising mortgage payments only serve to make people demand higher wages and are reflected in the Retail Price Index. The extreme boom of 1988 was set off by a combination of easy credit, low interest rates, and young couples entering the market. This cocktail is unlikely to be repeated. Lenders were stung by record possessions following their easy policy of 1988 and will be more selective in allocating mortgages.

Residential Property
1989–1993
The slump which afflicted the housing market from 1989 to 1993 was the worst in living memory. Prices in real terms fell dramatically. This recession was different from its predecessors for a number of reasons. First, its length was such as to create great uncertainty as to when it would end. Actual unemployment and the fear of unemployment undoubtedly prevented people

from moving home. Second, many people took on considerable personal debt in the late 1980's when it was easy to get credit. Rising property prices were at the heart of this phenomenon. Many remortgaged their homes in order to fulfil their dreams – getting builders in to undertake extensions, buying new furniture and new cars.

By 1992 "negative equity" – being lumbered with a mortgage which was worth far more than a home – was an all too familiar problem. It affected 1.5 million homeowners and brought the housing market to a virtual standstill. A key ingredient was inflation. In the mid 70's slump, real house prices fell but nominal house prices failed to because of runaway soaring inflation. In 1989–1993 low inflation meant that nominal prices had to fall. The value of many houses became less than the loan secured on them. Many people simply could not move house even if they wanted to.

Another significant occurrence was the rise in house possessions. Many people were pushed financially at the time as unemployment started to rise towards the 3 million mark. Once a house is possessed it has to be sold. The number coming onto the market was such that already falling prices were forced down further. In this climate, first-time buyers naturally wanted to wait until prices had hit rock bottom before entering the market.

By 1993 the signs were that the slump was slowly drawing to an end. Interest rates were at historically low levels. There was a feeling that house prices had hit their bottom and would start to pick up. Many houses were on the market waiting to be snapped up at affordable prices.

For a first time buyer opportunities were now plentiful. Even those people having to sell their own property could buy a relative bargain at the other end. Property was back as a sound investment!

Many commentators see the 90's as a decade of low inflation and lower interest rates than in the 70's and 80's. Increases in house prices in such a scenario are likely to be gradual, only increasing significantly over a long period. This generally is far preferable to the extreme boom/bust cycle of recent years.

WHAT DETERMINES THE PRICE OF HOUSES?

Like all prices, house prices are determined by the law of supply and demand: the greater is the demand the higher is the price and vice versa.

A number of factors influence the price of houses. These include: the size, location, plot size, condition and tenure (freehold or leasehold) of a property.

The state of the property market in a given area, including the strength of the local economy, the national economy, or interest rates, also have a crucial effect on prices.

Other important factors include how well an individual property is presented as well as seasonal price fluctuations.

Actual prices achieved in the market place (not asking prices which can be way over the true worth) are a good indication of what price is achievable. The more individual a property is the more difficult it is to accurately value: its value is what somebody is prepared to pay.

To obtain the best possible price for a home means that it needs to be exposed to the widest possible market: the more people that see it, the better the chance of getting a sale at the best price.

WHY SELLING AND MOVING UP MARKET IS SUCH A WISE THING TO DO

From your first home to your last the financial outlay involved will almost certainly continue to be the largest investment you make. With luck and care it should also be your most profitable.

The important point to make is that certain factors are present which create a general upward price tendency. Their existence dictates that over the longer term prices will continue to rise faster than earnings. Such factors include:

1. At any one time, there is almost always a mountain of mortgage funds available. Hence the stiff competition between the financial institutions to win over new mortgage holders who, in the case of the building societies, will be a main source of income.

2. As the population continues to increase so will the number of households.

3. The trend for there to be an increase in the availability of second incomes for mortgage applications.

4. The limited amount of land available for ongoing residential building.

5. The continuance of the tendency to further home ownership. It is estimated that almost 70 per cent of households have purchased their own home. In the 1980s, the Conservative government promoted the sale of council homes to tenants to stimulate greater home ownership.

Briefly, the advantages of home ownership are as follows.

(a) You can easily borrow against residential property and get tax relief on your mortgage payment.

(b) You can enjoy the benefits of your home each and every day you live there. This gives most of us great pride and a feeling of security and contentment.

(c) When you sell your home you normally incur *no* taxation of any kind.

(d) If your circumstances change you can always sell.

(e) In the early 1990s, people have been put off moving, but this should be less likely in the future.

KEY POINT

Selling your house and investing in a better residence will continue to be a very wise step to take.

It is unlikely that the extreme boom/slump period of the late eighties and early nineties will reoccur in the near future. Rises and falls in home prices are likely to be more moderate.

AVOID THE TWO HOME TRAP

Unless you are extremely wealthy, the worst trap you can fall into is to end up owning two homes. That will bring on all sorts of financial headaches. You'll probably have to take out a bridging loan to cover the extra cost of your new home. But if you're unable to sell your existing home and are still paying a mortgage on it, then the bridging loan will become a crippling debt very soon.

The golden rule should be not to commit yourself to buy any other property until you are certain that you can sell your own. That way, even if you have to take out a bridging loan, it will be of the closed type which is less risky.

Circumstances might dictate that you feel compelled to buy another property before selling your existing one. For instance, if you lived in the West Midlands and a change of job took you to Edinburgh.

In this situation, the tactics to adopt would be as follows.

First, put your house on the market as soon as you know a move elsewhere is required. That way, you give yourself the most possible time to sell.

Second, look to rent property in the area you're moving to until you have succeeded in selling your existing home. You should endeavour to make several trips to your new area, visiting local estate agents to find out how easy it is to get somewhere to live, whether rented or bought. Renting should work out cheaper than a bridging loan and has the further attraction that it will give you ample time to buy when you need to.

Third, reassess your selling strategy if you haven't managed to sell when the time approaches to move. You might be forced to drop your asking price. That could mean that you feel you are "losing" money, but your overall financial circumstances probably dictate that underselling is a necessary evil to avoid the millstone of two mortgages. Often, there's a psychological barrier over the price. Let's say your home is one of several semi-detached properties for sale in the range £80,000 to £85,000. Dropping down to around £78,000 could well stimulate an interest, especially if you took an advert to this effect in the local paper.

Finally, many people hold out for a certain price and until they get it resort to renting their old home. This approach has its pros and cons and you need to weigh up very carefully whether this is your chosen option.

On the plus side, it is better to rent out your former home than to leave it standing empty. The longer it is left unlived in, the harder it will be to sell. A cold empty house just won't appeal and any potential buyers will want to knock you down in price. Occupied, it's more secure from vandalism. Then there's the financial consideration that you'll be deriving an income from the rent which could go some way towards meeting the mortgage payments – although you will be liable to pay income tax on the rental income.

On the minus side, tenants could well take a shine to your property and be reluctant to move. You can get round this if you give an appropriate lease. You should also ensure that the terms of rent provide for visits by prospective buyers. Because you're not there, the house might not be in a spick and span condition and it could prove difficult to sell.

A WORD ON MORTGAGES

Unless you were fortunate enough to be able to buy your home outright, you'll already have some experience of a mortgage.

When you sell your home, the amount you receive will be used to pay off the outstanding debt. Almost certainly, you'll need to take out another mortgage on your intended new home.

I have covered this subject in depth in the companion volume, *Save Money Buying Your Home.* You need to be aware of several key points.

1. You might save money through taking out a new mortgage with your existing lender. But shop around. Equally you might get a better deal elsewhere.

2. If at all possible, avoid taking out a bridging loan which can become a crippling debt. Avoid open bridging loans, which are given before you have sold your own home. Otherwise you'll find yourself in the two home, two mortgage trap. If you have to take out a bridging loan, then the closed type (only given when you have sold your home) is best.

3. Look to pay as large a deposit as you can comfortably afford on your new home. Ideally, this should be around 20 to 30 per cent of the purchase price of a property. That way you could avoid the costs of an indemnity guarantee. But don't take out a mortgage which you will be constantly struggling

to pay. The end result could be possession.

4. If you intend to move house frequently – say every 5 years – avoid fixed rate mortgages. They aren't normally portable. Endowment and pension mortgages are best suited to frequent movers.

5. Where you have a pension or endowment type mortgage, ensure that your new lender is willing to accept the continuance of the policies. Should they refuse, find a lender who will.

6. Don't be persuaded to cash in an existing endowment policy to start a new one afresh. You'll be considerably out of pocket if you do.

HOW TO AVOID POSSESSION OF YOUR HOME

In 1991 88,000 UK homes were taken into possession by their mortgagees, the highest number ever. By 1993 the figure was still 58,000.

Analysts didn't have far to look for the cause. The tragic situation coincided with serious mortgage arrears with record numbers of borrowers falling between six months and a year behind in their scheduled payments.

Interest rates had been high for a long period while a very depressed property market prevented many people from selling their home and moving down market. In many cases, the fall in property prices was such that mortgages exceeded the current value of homes creating "negative equity." Also, tax relief remained at a limit of £30,000, whereas 3 out of 4 new mortgages were for more than this.

All of this followed on from the mid 80's when conditions for a housing boom were perfect: falling interest rates, easy credit, large numbers of young couples entering the market, and a tax system favouring home ownership.

The message is clear: do not overstretch yourself financially when taking on a mortgage. Put down as much as you can. It's better to borrow 80 per cent of the value of a house than 90 per cent. That way, if you do get into difficulties, your lender is liable to be patient for longer, giving you more breathing space.

Possibly you will already have made this mistake. Other typical circumstances leading to mortgage repayment difficulties are: redundancy, a significant and sudden drop in earnings, and marital difficulties.

Whatever the reason for the problem, you should talk to your lender as soon as possible. The longer you leave it the worse the problem will become. For instance, after three months of non payments some lenders impose an additional fee (around 2 per cent of the total outstanding). Don't indulge in wishful thinking and somehow believe matters will resolve themselves. They just won't. Even if you can't afford to pay the full monthly mortgage repayment, it's best to pay something, which at least demonstrates to your lender that you are making an effort.

Bear in mind that the lender will only decide to go for possession as a last resort and will prefer to pursue all other options first. The steps a lender can take to help vary according to personal circumstances, the type of mortgage, and the cause of the payment problem.

Sometimes it is possible to peg payments at a lower interest rate for a period of time. A lender may even be prepared to suspend payments for a short period. Arrears balances can also be added on to the main loan in certain circumstances.

If you have lost your job it may be possible to get assistance from the DSS. Government help with mortgages is available if you are on Income Support. Again, your lender may be able to point you in the right direction. Note, however, that no payments are made for endowment or mortgage policies connected with the loan. Should you or your partner have savings above a certain amount you cannot receive any Income Support. Details are available at DSS offices or your local Citizens' Advice Bureau.

It may be worth you taking on a temporary part-time job or considering taking in lodgers to ease your difficulties. When interest rates were high in the 1980's rent from a lodger using the spare room was an important device to help meet mortgage payments.

If you do decide to let a room or rooms you need to inform your mortgage lender. Normally, they won't object. But be careful not to start running a bed and breakfast establishment. Then you'll be considered to be operating a commercial venture, meaning that the terms of your mortgage would have to alter. Remember, too, that where the income from lodgers exceeds a certain level, it should be declared and will be liable to tax. Provided lodgers share meals and are treated as part of the family, the house should escape Capital Gains Tax when you sell. But if part of your house is *let*, then some Capital Gains Tax may possibly fall due.

If your circumstances become

absolutely desperate, you could try letting your home out for a period and either go to rented accommodation or stay with relatives or friends. Taking out an Assured Shorthold lease will ensure that the house becomes available to you again when you require it.

In the case of an endowment mortgage, try to persuade the life assurance company to temporarily freeze endowment payments. Most will consider doing this for up to a year. If the endowment policy has been running for some time, it could be possible to cash it in for a useful amount of money (though the amount will vary from company to company) and then to use this to reduce the size of the mortgage.

Too many people aren't aware of the full implications of voluntary possession. On average around 40 per cent of possessions are voluntary. But, as often as not, handing in the house keys to a lender won't end the difficulties. First, if you fail to consult your lender, legal action could follow. Second, lenders are under no obligation to sell the property immediately and might decide to wait until the market picks up to their liking. Until the house is sold, you will still have to meet your mortgage payments. Third, it is possible that the house will be sold at auction

for a much lower figure than you might have raised through a personal sale. Last, your local council, perhaps with a long housing waiting list, could deem that you have made yourself "voluntarily homeless" and feel no obligation to rehouse you.

To secure a forced possession, your lender has to obtain a Court Order. This will involve your case being heard in court. Here, your best move would be to seek advice from your local Citizens' Advice Bureau, who will have a free debt-counselling service or may be able to direct you on to a Money Advice Centre. As well as advising you, the staff can negotiate directly with your lender with a view to reaching an agreement. In such an event, the Order will be suspended. There could also be schemes whereby you sell your home to a housing association but remain living in it for a rent. At some future date, it might be possible to buy your home back.

If your case does come to court, be sure to attend in person should you be unable to afford a lawyer to act on your behalf. This won't guarantee that you'll win a reprieve, but it's your last best chance. Failure to make a case at all will almost certainly lead the court to endorse the possession. Then you'll be obliged to leave your home by the date given in the Order. And, as with voluntary possessions, you'll remain tied to your mortgage until the house is sold. Moreover, in both types of possessions, if the property is sold for less than you owe, you'll be liable for the difference.

Should your house be possessed it may make it very difficult for you to get a mortgage in the future. Where an eviction results from a Court Order, the possession is recorded on a central register, operated by the Registry Trust, which is the source for all the main credit reference agencies. Also, the Council of Mortgage Lenders has begun its own register of possessions to cover voluntary cases. If you have any complaints about possession then you can contact the Office of the Building Society Ombudsman (see Addresses P. 92).

Selling your house yourself and moving down market or into rented accommodation, is your best option if you don't see things improving. You're likely to get a much better price than if you opt for voluntary possession or delay acting until compulsory possession is upon you. You may even be able to move down market and have any negative equity added into a new, smaller, mortgage.

Presentation is all important in achieving the best price and if you vacate your home then it can only deteriorate. There's a saying that "Nothing's as cold as an empty house." It's not literally true, but the longer a dwelling stands empty, the harder it will become to sell it at a reasonable price. Dirty windows, cobwebbed walls, uncut grass, sprawling weeds – these are all weapons which a buyer will use to knock down the selling price. Worse still, your home might be vandalised or uninvited guests could move in.

Building societies can take over a year to sell a possessed home and on average they only achieve about 70 per cent of the open market valuation. What you must do is to recognise your problems at an early stage and act (sell) before possession becomes your only option.

Finally, on the principle that "prevention is better than cure", you could insure yourself against loss of income through being made redundant. Redundancy packages and income protection plans are available. There are also specific redundancy plans for homeowners. Some building societies also offer mortgage payment protection schemes. Remember, though, that you probably won't be able to claim on this type of insurance if you are made redundant soon after taking out a policy. Nor do they usually cover voluntary redundancy. The policies are useful as a temporary respite, though your mortgage repayments will be met for a limited period only.

LEGAL ASPECTS

The legal niceties on buying a home are covered in some depth in the companion volume *Save Money Buying Your Home*. Here we will briefly consider the procedure from the viewpoint of the seller, but in the majority of cases a seller will also be buying a house at the same time as selling one.

Once you and your estate agent are happy that you have a buyer ready, willing and able to go ahead and you have negotiated an acceptable price, it is necessary for you to convey (i.e. legally transfer your ownership in your house to that of your proposed buyer) in return for the money agreed.

The system of selling your home is different in Scotland and we will be considering this later on as a separate item.

FIRST STEPS

By the time you are ready to instruct your solicitor you should have obtained quotations and know which solicitor you will be using.

The first step your solicitor will take upon receiving your instructions to sell will be to obtain the title deeds from either you directly or your bank if you own your house outright, or from the lender if you have a mortgage.

The next step your solicitor will take is to prepare a contract of sale and send this to your buyer's solicitor.

DEALING WITH YOUR BUYER'S ENQUIRIES

One of the first actions of your buyer's solicitor will involve him in making some preliminary enquiries (enquiries before contract) directed towards your solicitor. These will be on a standard form and you will be required to answer certain questions about the property you are selling.

Questions will include what fixtures and fittings you have agreed to leave, whether you know of any adverse rights affecting the property, what services you have etc. At the same time, your buyer's solicitor will be carrying out a local search on your home with the local council. This asks whether any development schemes, road widening projects, or other planning matters, rights of way etc. affect the property.

OTHER THINGS YOUR BUYER WILL BE DOING

Your buyer, if he needs a loan, will probably have commissioned a valuation or survey, or the building society will have on his behalf. Normally this will be carried out a few days after the solicitors have been instructed in the sale of your property.

TRANSACTION

In 1990, the TransAction scheme was set up by the Law Society in relation to property transactions in the UK outside Scotland. The procedures adopted by the scheme (the Protocol), is now in its third edition. The scheme was designed to streamline the conveyancing process by the use of standard contracts and forms enabling your solicitor to focus on the distinctive characteristics of the transaction and your individual needs. The take up of the Protocol has been very patchy, and some areas of the country do not adopt the procedures at all.

Having decided to move, and having chosen your solicitor, discuss the TransAction scheme with him.

EXCHANGE OF CONTRACTS

Once you and your buyer are happy with the contract, the searches and the pre-contract enquiries are completed, and your buyer has received a satisfactory offer of a mortgage, then contracts can be exchanged, at which point the deal becomes binding on both parties and neither can drop out.

It is important, therefore, if you are buying another house as well that your solicitor exchanges contracts simultaneously on the home you are buying to avoid the problem of your proposed purchase falling through and you finding yourself having to vacate your present house with nowhere to move to.

On exchange of contracts a deposit, normally amounting to 10 per cent of the purchase price, is paid to your solicitor.

After Exchange of Contracts

After exchanging contracts but before completion, which will normally happen within 28 days of exchange, your solicitor still has various things to do.

Your buyer's solicitor will be checking over the title of your property to ensure that you are the legal owner and can actually sell the property. If there are any matters that your buyer's solicitor is not happy with he will send written questions (requisitions on title) to your solicitor.

The conveyance or transfer deed is the deed that passes your interest in the property to the buyer. A draft of this is sent to your solicitor from the buyer's solicitor after exchange of contracts. Once approved your buyer's solicitor will engross the deed and provide for the balance of the purchase price to be made ready. If all is well, completion takes place and your buyer takes possession of the property and receives the title deeds in exchange for the balance of the purchase price. At this stage your solicitor redeems (pays off) your mortgage before accounting to you.

LEGAL FEES ON THE SALE OF A HOUSE

The legal fees involved in selling a house are mainly the costs for your solicitor's time: there is no stamp duty, search fee, or land registry fees to meet – as would be the case if you were buying a house.

The following table shows that by ringing around different solicitors for quotations, fees can vary considerably and you could save yourself quite an amount of money.

SELLING A HOME IN SCOTLAND

In Scotland you will need to let your solicitor know of your intention to sell your home even before it goes on the market. Your solicitor needs to check the title deeds of your property. He will also need to obtain local authority searches to ensure your home is not affected by any local authority proposals.

Most houses in Scotland are sold by solicitors and not by estate agents. However, Solicitors' Property Centres do not actively "sell" houses. They tend to wait for a buyer to turn up. This perhaps partly explains why estate agents are becoming increasingly popular in Scotland!

Many properties will be on display at the local solicitors' property centre where, normally, a standard registration fee is charged. The property will be displayed in the centre until sold.

An estate agent's or solicitor's opinion of value is normally supplied free of charge but check on this when making any valuation appointment. Many properties are advertised at "Offers Over" a certain figure.

In Scotland there is no such thing as an offer subject to contract. In the rest of the UK both you or a buyer can withdraw from a sale with no penalty whatsoever up until the point that contracts are exchanged. But in Scotland if you formally accept an offer this is not the case.

A prospective buyer will very often have a building society valuation or more detailed survey carried out before submitting

LEGAL FEES QUOTED ON A HOUSE SALE ONLY AT £80,000

	Solicitor A	B	C
Birmingham	£460	160	290
Bristol	300	250	350
Southampton	265	300	330

N.B. VAT needs to be added.

any offer. In Scotland search dues (equivalent to the local search fees in the rest of the UK) are paid for by you, the vendor, and undertaken by your solicitor.

The offer, of course, forms the basis of your contract of sale and will contain a large number of conditions. It is, therefore, important that you discuss the offer in detail with your solicitor before accepting and becoming bound by it.

It is important that you provide a list of everything that you are leaving and the date by which you wish to move (the entry date).

Sometimes a number of letters are required to adjust the details of your and your buyer's contractual obligations. Only when all the conditions are agreed is there a binding contract. The offer and letters are called "the missives".

When there are several parties interested in buying your house it is normal practice to fix a "Closing Date" for offers. Your solicitor will advise you on this.

There is normally a period of time between you accepting an offer and the date your buyer is to take entry. In the meantime it is normal for a buyer to have access, although keys will not be formally handed over until the full price has been paid to your solicitor.

SELLING YOUR HOME: KEY MONEY, MAKING AND SAVING POINTS

1. When considering the option of selling, achieving the best price in the shortest possible time should be your main goal. You have more chance of achieving this if your house is exposed to the widest possible market.

2. When selling your house remember it is very important to focus your mind on the difference between the prices you sell and buy for. If you can get a bigger reduction on the home you are buying, it *may* be worth selling your current home for slightly less than you would have liked.

3. Try and sell in the first half of the year if at all possible.

4. Recognise your strengths and weaknesses and relate these to the climate in which you try to sell – a sellers' market or a buyers' market.

5. Remember there is no precise fixed price for a house. Do all you can to ensure that you maximise the amount that you sell your home for.

6. Look to avoid having two homes. Sell your own first before buying another property.

7. Avoid possession if at all possible.

8. Negotiate on solicitors fees. Ring around and compare quotations. Very substantial savings are there to be made.

9. Always arrange with your solicitor that you will be kept notified in writing of everything that is going on.

10. Consider using the TransAction scheme but make sure you discuss this fully with your solicitor first.

AND THEY'RE ALL SO REASONABLY PRICED ...

WE'LL SHOW THEM THE GARDEN
SOME OTHER TIME ...

SECTION 2: DEALING WITH OFFERS AND NEGOTIATING

This section looks at:

DEALING WITH OFFERS AND NEGOTIATING

There are a number of situations which can arise in the process of selling your house where you will need to negotiate. These are:

- Negotiating on the fees and the service you will get from your estate agent.

- Negotiating on the fees and service you will get from your solicitor.

- Negotiating with your prospective buyer on price and terms. This will certainly be down to you if you are selling your own house, or where you are selling through an estate agent but are happy to negotiate direct with your prospective purchaser rather than refer to your estate agent. Many estate agents, however, will prefer to do the negotiating.

NEGOTIATIONS: GENERAL PRINCIPLES

Negotiation may be defined as "discussing with a view to mutual settlement". As a house seller the people you will negotiate with will want the opposite to what you want. The estate agent will be looking to obtain the best fee possible where you will be looking to pay the lowest fee that is commensurate with the best selling service you can afford. Again, the solicitor will be looking to extract a sizeable fee in return for his services, while you will want to pay as little as he will accept for doing his work properly. Finally, a prospective buyer will want to acquire your home if at all possible at a lower figure than you ideally want.

You must be firm yet flexible and prepared to compromise. Meeting halfway is often the outcome of such discussions, but be prepared to back out if your objectives are being totally thrown out of the window. It is always important to maintain a pleasant disposition when negotiating.

That way, even if you don't resolve your differences immediately the other party will be willing to come back another day. Remember also to leave something for the other person to negotiate on. In other words, don't burn all your bridges at the first meeting unless you have decided immediately that the other party is intent on riding roughshod over your interests.

To negotiate well you must be aware of the strengths and weaknesses of your position. If you are negotiating with an estate agent for example, you are likely to get better terms from him when the house market is moving quite well. This context will ensure that the estate agent is anxious to replace those houses on his books that he has sold, and will be keen to have your business. On the other hand, if houses are not selling at all well, and half of the homes in your street are for sale, you will have a much weaker hand. In a bad market you may well have to be more flexible on your price than in a good selling market.

Try not to close any doors. For example, if a low offer for your home comes in, avoid the temptation to dismiss it out of hand. Often this is only a starting gambit on the part of the buyer, who wants to test out your position. Often he will be prepared to increase his bid.

Do not make concessions all

at once. If somebody offers £10,000 less than the asking price of your house, you should not accept the offer immediately, no matter how desperate you might be to sell. Should you do so the buyer may well conclude that he could obtain your home for even less, and will then come up with an even lower offer. As in life, we all like to struggle for our achievements.

Never reveal to a prospective buyer your anxiety to achieve a sale. This might be for financial reasons – say if you have taken out a bridging loan. If you do, it will invariably result in a lower offer for your home.

Generally speaking your first buyer will give you the best deal. Obviously this can only be confirmed with the benefit of hindsight. The person who is likely to offer the highest price for a house is the person most keen on buying it. This is an area where the professional judgement of an experienced estate agent can be crucial. It takes intuition to tell whether the first offer is fortuitous and good and should be accepted quickly and clearly. Or whether to turn it down and hope to do better.

CASE STUDY: KEY POINT

The classic case of a first buyer offering the best price occurred in my experience a few years ago. One of the finest properties in the area came on the market and was pitched for a time at the hopeful figure of £217,000. The seller had committed himself to buying another property, and a quick sale was being looked for. Within two days a professional in the town decided he would buy the house and was prepared to go ahead. To prove his enthusiasm he was even ready to exchange contracts within a month and to take out a bridging loan.

The only condition from the buyer's viewpoint was that the curtains and carpets, which were of a very high quality, were included in the deal. The owner was not wiling to accept a penny less than £5,000 for these items. This insistence was enough to kill the deal, and the buyer dropped out. Several months went by without a sale being achieved. In the end the seller had to part with his house for the knock down price of £206,000 which included the cherished carpets and curtains! By this time he had also incurred bridging finance and some considerable worry into the bargain.

THE IMPORTANCE OF CURTAINS AND CARPETS

In negotiations to buy properties reference may be made to fixtures and fittings, especially curtains and carpets. Fixtures like these, if they are acceptable to the purchasers, are of far greater value to them than to you because of the potential for saving money, keeping them rather than buying new.

Should you be selling such fixtures second hand rather than taking them with you to your new home, then your house buyer is likely to give you the best price. Removing them should be avoided where possible since there could be problems in taking them out, and alterations will be required if you are intending to reuse them.

By the same token, the buyer (unless a first-time buyer is involved) is unlikely to want to bring fixtures and fittings from their old home, at least in their entirety. Provided, therefore, that the purchaser likes your existing fixtures and fittings you will be in a strong bargaining position to obtain the selling price you want while at the same time offering the buyer substantial savings through avoiding having to buy new fixtures and fittings. Have this factor in the back of your mind.

WHAT MAKES A GOOD BUYER?

When selling your house it is worth considering what type of buyers you may come across and which are the best type.

FIRST-TIME BUYER

First-time buyers with a mortgage arranged in principle are often excellent buyers. It is possible that they will be a couple looking to get married in the near future, a factor which will make them anxious to buy so long as the terms are right and they like your home.

Try and ask for confirmation of their mortgage offer or when their surveyor is likely to call to carry out the valuation on your house. Problems can arise with first-time buyers especially when they are borrowing a large amount of the purchase price – say over 90 per cent. If your house is then down valued by the building society, difficulties can arise. This is a very good reason to always agree the fixtures and fittings separately from the house price.

A BUYER WHO HAS BRIDGING FINANCE

Such buyers are often in a very good position to proceed straight away. Most commonly the buyer's firm will be prepared to provide the finance. Again, ask to see a confirming letter where appropriate.

A BUYER WHO HAS ALREADY EXCHANGED CONTRACTS ON THE SALE OF HIS OWN HOUSE

Such a buyer has a definite sale and provided he can obtain a mortgage he should be able to go ahead quickly.

A CASH BUYER

Be warned that many people claim to be cash buyers when they are nothing of the sort. A true cash buyer is somebody who can pay whatever your price is without a mortgage and is *not* dependent on selling his existing house.

THE BUYER WITH A HOUSE TO SELL

In this situation you should always keep your house on the market until the buyer is in a position to go ahead. There is always the possibility that he may not sell or that he may in the end decide not to move after all. By all means, exchange names and addresses and keep the person advised, but under no circumstances commit yourself to sell. Try and establish how long the buyer's house has been on the market. If it has been on offer for some time then clearly there is a problem in achieving a sale and you should be even more cautious.

THE BUYER WHO SAYS HE HAS "SOLD" HIS OWN HOUSE SUBJECT TO CONTRACT

This set of circumstances is very commonplace and so you should expect to face such a scenario. Here you, or your estate agent,

must check down the chain to ensure that a buyer fitting into one of the first four categories is clearly identified.

The longer the chain is the greater chance there is of things going wrong.

THE ADVANTAGES OF NEGOTIATING THROUGH AN ESTATE AGENT

Many people, whether buying or selling houses, are very reluctant to negotiate directly. This is perfectly understandable. A good estate agent will be trained to negotiate and find common ground. It is also important for you to have time and space between the making and the conclusion of a deal, which an estate agent provides.

The estate agent will also be highly experienced in checking the "chain" of your buyer to ensure he or she is in a position to go ahead. This involves establishing that all parties in a transaction have sold their house to buyers who can go ahead. All parties must also have a mortgage agreed in principle, if indeed they require a mortgage. If you are selling yourself you will need to verify this information, but it could be more difficult for you than for an estate agent.

THE VALUATION AND SURVEY OF YOUR HOME

It is likely that whoever agrees to buy your house will have either a valuation or survey done. Banks and building societies will insist on at least a basic inspection and valuation before agreeing to lend money on a residential property, and only an unwise cash buyer would go ahead and buy somewhere without first having a valuation and survey undertaken.

The types of valuation and survey that may be involved for a prospective buyer on your home include:

BASIC REPORT AND VALUATION

This is based on a normal building society type of report and includes guidance on the value of property, together with a *basic* statement on the condition of the property. It is not vastly detailed and is confined to the basic structure only.

HOME BUYERS' SURVEY AND VALUATION

Based on the recommendations of the Royal Institution of Chartered Surveyors or Incorporated Society of Valuers and Auctioneers, and prepared by a chartered surveyor or incorporated valuer, the report is several pages in length and is designed for the prospective purchaser of a house giving guidance for most of the building with regard to basic structure, roof, walls, windows, internal condition, drainage, paths etc. The property's services are not normally tested but advice will be given if the surveyor is not satisfied with their condition and functioning. In this instance, he will often recommend their inspection by a specialist. A report of this type is mainly for properties under the age of eighty years of age and of residential nature only.

FULL REPORT AND SURVEY

This is a detailed and very comprehensive report on the property with specialists being involved to test various aspects of the house if necessary.

Once the surveyor has inspected your house, the problems which could arise are:

a) The property is down valued in price.

b) Repairs are shown to be necessary.

c) The property is down valued because of carpets and curtains being included.

It is estimated that only 15 per cent of the property buying public have a survey done, so in fact around eight out of ten people buying a property rely on the mortgage valuation alone.

Should a prospective buyer come back to you claiming the house has been down valued and try to renegotiate the price previously agreed on the basis of the surveyor's conclusions, there are a number of options open to you. My own strategy for dealing with this situation is as follows.

First, tell the buyer that a mortgage valuation is not the same thing as an open market value. The true value of a house, or anything else come to that, is what somebody else is prepared to pay for it – no more, no less.

Second, ask to see a copy of the valuation report so that you know precisely what has been said about your home. This will serve to clarify and confirm any criticisms that have been made.

If a buyer is adamant about a price reduction then you have to decide whether to accept or reject their revised bid. To a large degree your decision will be influenced by market conditions and specifically by the interest that has been shown in your home.

Where things may get difficult is in a situation where a buyer needs a very large mortgage, say even as much as 100 per cent. A down valuation by the surveyor means that the buyer simply can't get a mortgage to cover the purchase price of your house.

The building society is not permitted to lend more than the valuation says that the property is worth. A get out here could be another valuation (though this will cost him so the buyer must be keen). Surveyors do tend to err on the side of caution.

Where repairs are necessary arising from a survey you should respond that the price set may already be judged to reflect this. The catalogue of necessary repairs may come as a surprise, but needn't have done. If you had used a qualified estate agent to value your home in the first place he could have pointed out some of the problem areas in advance where they existed, which could have made the process easier. The more you understand what is happening, and anticipate any problems in advance, the easier you are going to feel in your mind and the less traumatic the selling process will prove to be.

In a good market, or where you are in a strong position, you can stand firm. In any other situation it may be necessary to make a contribution to some of the repairs by reducing the price slightly. Always try and negotiate. If the buyer asks you to pay for the total costs of repairs, counter by offering to pay a third and remarking that the repairs will have the effect of making the house more valuable immediately.

Because of problems such as those described above, it is

important that you keep your home on the open market until all the surveys and valuations have been carried out.

SHOWING PEOPLE AROUND YOUR HOME

The main point to make when showing people around your home is always to be very pleasant and friendly. People do buy people first and whatever else second.

Of course, somebody is not going to buy your home if it is not what they want, but there are many situations where a potential buyer would have bought a particular property if the seller had been more courteous and friendly.

Try not to breathe down people's necks whilst they are looking around. If they want you to show them round fine, but only one person should do the showing; crowding four people in a small room can make the room appear smaller than it actually is.

Ensure that your home is as well presented as possible (see the later section, Presentation and Maintenance P. 69) and remember that ideally children and pets should neither be seen nor heard as both can destroy the buying mood.

Try to answer all questions put to you as truthfully as you can. If a prospective buyer thinks you are not being honest or are being deliberately misleading they will probably be put off.

After the prospective buyer has looked around, be prepared to progress the sale. Do not offer alcoholic drinks when you may be finalising a sale. Instead, just offer coffee or tea which won't break the buying mood.

Be well prepared. Have property details to hand, photographs of your home taken at different times of the year, details of heating costs etc. Ensure that there are no obvious distractions such as loud music or a blaring television set.

If the viewers wish to make an offer refer them to your estate agent if you are using one.

Be aware of the security aspect when showing people around. Most people viewing property are, of course, perfectly genuine but it pays to be cautious. Be sure to know something about prospective purchasers before showing them how the burglar alarm works or where the safe is! Ensure too that you and your estate agent have the name, the address, telephone and car registration number of everyone who looks at your home.

If you are using an estate agent and you prefer accompanied viewings these should be made via the agent. If you are not at home at the time of viewing or if you are selling a vacant home then, for security reasons, do ensure that keys are kept secure at an estate agents' office and not given out to prospective buyers and others.

TIPS ON MOVING

Once you have sold your home and are to move out the chances are you will be moving on to another house, whether it is one you have bought or is rented accommodation. Basically, two choices lie before you: either to move yourself by borrowing or hiring a van; or hiring a firm of removers to remove your house contents for you.

Should you elect to move yourself then, unless you or a friend happen to possess a large enough van, your expenses will involve the cost of van hire and petrol. Obviously, the further you have to move the greater your expense will be. Depending on the extent and nature of your possessions, several trips will be involved. Where both long distances and many journeys are called for, not to mention the hard work involved in loading and unloading the van, you ought to consider the alternative of hiring a removal firm.

If you decide to go to a firm of removers you may have several possible options, from the staff packing all of your belongings to them just loading and delivering what you have already packed.

The key point is first to obtain several quotations on the price for moving. It is better if the firm can send a representative to your home to "assess" the job in hand.

A further useful tip is that if you are moving from a large town to a smaller one you should carefully think about the cost of hiring the removers in the latter since they could well offer a cheaper service.

Also bear in mind the fact that certain times, such as at the end of the week, can be particularly busy for removal firms. It is best to check out and avoid these.

THE CONTRACT

It is important that you read the contract for the move very carefully. Be clear what the firm is stating it will do and what the procedure is if the removal men happen to damage any of your belongings while in course of removal.

Many firms insert clauses into their contracts limiting their liability for loss or damage to very small amounts indeed. Many contracts also contain an arbitration clause which means that if a dispute arises you cannot take the firm to court.

INSURANCE

Before moving check with your home contents insurer that you are covered. Alternatively you may need to arrange some "one off" cover to take care of your removal.

KEY POINT

It pays to shop around. Costs vary greatly. In the early 1990's a Which? report was revealing. Four removal firms were asked to quote for a removal within London. The difference between the highest and lowest tenders was as much as £156! From Edinburgh to Birmingham the difference was even greater – £532!

DEALING WITH OFFERS AND NEGOTIATING: KEY MONEY MAKING AND SAVING POINTS

1. Once you have sold your own house, and solicitors are instructed and everything is fine with the chain, you are in the strongest position to negotiate on the property you want to buy.

2. Remember that very often your first buyer will give you the best deal.

3. Never disclose anything to a prospective buyer that shows you are desperate to sell.

4. Many fixtures and fittings are likely to be of much greater value to your prospective buyer than to you. It may be expensive for your buyer to recarpet immediately, especially if they are mortgaged to the hilt, so this can be a useful bargaining counter providing you don't overplay your hand.

5. To avoid problems when the surveyor calls for your buyer's building society/bank valuation, negotiate all fixtures and fittings separately from the house price.

SECTION 3: YOUR CHOICE OF SELLING METHOD

This section looks at:

HOW DO YOU SELL YOUR HOME?

This is a simple enough question to pose. There are however three possible answers.

1. The first option, and that chosen by the majority, is to sell your property through an estate agent. Under this heading fall independent companies

and those owned by large institutions, (there were many takeovers in the property boom of the 1980s) such as building societies and insurance companies.

2. A second option is provided by property shops, which claim to offer similar facilities to an estate agent but at a fraction of the cost. Although many property shops were short lived (for instance, the Woolworths chain), others, such as Seekers, are very well established in certain locations. They remain, therefore, a credible alternative and we will be looking into their advantages and disadvantages.

3. Finally, you can sell privately. This might be to a friend or acquaintance or, alternatively, you may wish to pursue the option of selling your property to a wider audience. Provided that you know what you are doing, this holds the attraction of saving a lot of money. In practice, as we will see, self-selling may not be quite so easy as it appears at first. Should you choose to go it alone, then you will obviously need to go about selling in the right manner to maximise your chances of a successful sale. Later on I will give a number of very valuable tips for those who decide to take this route.

WHO DO YOU CHOOSE TO SELL YOUR HOME?

The question would be far harder to answer without the benefit of this book. Preparation and planning is important in any walk of life; but it is absolutely crucial when what is almost certainly your most vital asset is going to be sold. In other words, at this preliminary stage you must put a little bit of work and effort into the venture. In the longer term you are likely to be well rewarded for some careful planning and proper weighing of the options.

Because estate agents remain by far the most popular route for selling property, they will be dealt with first and in the most detail. Not all estate agents are the same. Using the "correct" individual and company can make a significant difference to the price which you eventually obtain for your home. Paying £2,000 plus VAT to sell a

£100,000 property may seem to be steep; but if by choosing the wrong estate agent you end up with only £95,000 it is cheap.

In my experience, good estate agents obtain far better prices than any of the other methods of sale. Added advantages which they bring are convenience and security – they arrange viewings of the property and accompany prospective buyers where required. They will also be able to offer you good advice if things go wrong.

Whatever method you decide to sell by, look through the estate agency checklist (see P. 57) and arrange to have at least two or three free valuations carried out. Even before doing this you should study the property advertisements in your local newspaper. From these it may be clear which estate agents are selling the most, and you might glean an idea of the types of property that they specialise in. Above all, the way they present houses (so crucial to a successful sale) should be a major influence in determining which estate agent you choose.

Your next step should be a tour of your area in search of "For Sale" notices. That way, if you don't already know it, you'll find out just which estate agents are selling the most property. It could well also be that the more successful are able to offer the most competitive fees.

After this, indulge in some window shopping by viewing the property adverts in an estate agent's window. By now, you'll have a good 'feel' for the estate agent you prefer. At the same time, remember that the outside appearance can be deceptive. Actually go in to estate agents' offices and request some property details even if you are moving out of the branch area. How were you received? Are the staff keen? Enthusiasm can help to sell houses.

ESTATE AGENTS

THE AMAZING TRUTH ABOUT "NO SALE NO CHARGE" FROM THE AGENT'S VIEWPOINT

"No Sale No Charge" offers big advantages to estate agents. It is easy to administer – no more of those laborious records of how often a property is advertised, for instance. It is also a good marketing tool, on a par with High Street shops who draw in customers with the promise of '0 per cent interest' on their goods.

The idea of paying nothing if you do not sell (or payment by results) is sound. It works in this way. The agent allocates a sum for advertising. Let us suppose this is £500 a week for a page in a newspaper (it could of course be much higher or lower depending on the particular publication and its circulation). The main point is that no matter how long it takes to sell a particular property or how many homes are withdrawn in a given period the agent still has a fixed budget set aside for advertising. The regular newspaper spot will probably continue as long as the agent has a no sale no charge policy. What will change is the layout of the page and the prominence given to particular properties.

How can you influence the advertising process in these circumstances? Generally it is the agent who chooses how often a property is advertised. Arrange with the agent to whom you have given selling instructions that he advertises your home at specified intervals – each week, every fortnight or some other arrangement you are happy with.

Another point well worth noting is that in many cases the estate agent can decide which properties he would like a special feature on. This is a very eye-catching advert which will attract maximum attention. Ask your agent to request such a feature from the newspaper shortly after your home first goes on the market.

If the deal is that given a successful sale you will pay a fee *plus* advertising costs, be sure to clear up in advance exactly what you will have to pay. Specifically, ask the agent if the advertising rate is the net rate which they themselves pay the newspaper. Some estate agents make extra money by loading the actual costs to them of advertising and erecting the for sale board.

ESTATE AGENCY FEES

A key point to remember is that not all estate agents are the same when it comes to fees. But you should also consider that a good estate agent will obtain the maximum possible price for your property. The extra could be several thousand pounds; at the very least, it will net you hundreds of pounds more. As you read on, therefore, bear these two considerations in mind. At the end of the day, it is what you actually receive net of the estate agent's fee which is all important.

It may come as a surprise to learn that British estate agency fees are among the lowest in the world. Fees generally range between ½ and 2½ per cent. Elsewhere fees are much higher. In the United States the average ranges between 5 and 8 per cent (and can be as much as 10 per cent). Spain charges at similar levels while in Australia the government supports a 6 per cent fee.

Add VAT to U.K. agents' fees figures to finalise costs. Remember also that the fee structure will vary from one part of the country to another. The South is dearest.

TYPICAL BRITISH ESTATE AGENT'S FEES

Sale Price	Fee at 1%	Fee at 1½%	Fee at 2%	Fee at 2½%
£40,000	400	600	800	1,000
£70,000	700	1,050	1,400	1,750
£100,000	1,000	1,500	2,000	2,500
£150,000	1,500	2,250	3,000	3,750
£200,000	2,000	3,000	4,000	5,000

Here you can expect to pay 2–2½ per cent inclusive of advertising, boards etc. on a no sale no charge basis. By contrast, if you are in the North fees are likely to be lower, at between 1 and 1½ per cent but plus all the advertisements. In many cases the two types of estate agency charges are likely to co-exist side by side.

How Estate Agents Fees Vary

I carried out a survey of estate agents in areas throughout the United Kingdom, telephoning a number of offices to see what sort of fees they charged for selling a house at £80,000. It is quite clear that in many places you can save considerable sums of money just by ringing around. If you wanted to negotiate further, the time to do so is when the property has been valued. However, your success in negotiating may be influenced, of course, by how saleable the estate agent judges your home to be.

It was interesting to note during the research for this survey that in some cities, such as Birmingham and its surrounding towns, there is a mix of estate agents which charge a fee plus all costs including photographs etc., some that charge a fee plus only advertising, and some who charge an all inclusive fee and operate no sale no charge.

In some areas, especially the North, it may be that you cannot find an estate agent who operates on a no sale no charge basis, but you will find that there is still scope to negotiate on the fees.

Fees Quoted

Fees will almost certainly vary from agent to agent. They will also be determined by market conditions. In a fast moving market when houses are easily sold, selling agents are likely to be more flexible on fees. As we will see, your agent or advisers can negotiate for you on the price of your house, but in this area you have to negotiate for yourself.

It may be that your preferred estate agent is too dear. Here, you might telephone him and propose to deal with him only so long as he is willing to come down on his fee. He may well agree, but you should be prepared for him to hold firm.

At the same time, you should not regard the fee as the be all and end all. Other considerations may well be more important. Be prepared to negotiate on fees and consider suggesting a fixed sum rather than a percentage if you prefer.

What an Estate Agent will Charge

Obviously, as shown by the above figures, enlisting the services of an estate agent to sell your property is not a cheap proposition no matter where you are. But, you should not consider the fee in isolation. Rather view it within the overall perspective of what you may get for your home.

You must be prepared to bargain with the estate agent. There is frequently ample scope to negotiate a lower fee. All too often people just do not quibble over the fee level but readily accept it. By doing so they may be missing the opportunity to make valuable savings. Do be realistic, though. An estate agent might be prepared to knock some money off to secure your business, but he is most unlikely to slash his prices by any more than a few hundred pounds.

Now you know what you can get, view the issue in relation to the estate agency checklist on page 57 and follow my advice.

It is important that the meeting with the estate agent takes place in a good atmosphere. Strike a balance between being fairly firm while at the same time remaining pleasant and reasonable. The common ground between you is that both parties want to sell the property. Do not, therefore, treat the estate agent

TOWN/AREA	FEES QUOTED %		
	Estate Agent A	B	C
Bristol	2.5 (inclusive)	2 (inc.)	1.5 (inc.)
Southampton	2.5 (3% multiple agy)	1.75 (inc.)	1 (inc.)
Birmingham	1 (inclusive)	1.5 (exc.)	2.25 (inc.)
Edinburgh	1.5 (exclusive)	1 (exc.)	.75 (exc.)
Liverpool	1 (inclusive)	1.5 (exc.)	2 (inc.)
Cardiff	1 (inclusive)	1.5 (inc.)	2 (inc.)
Belfast	1.5 (inclusive)	.75 (exc.)	1 (exc.)

as though he were a salesman trying to sell something that you don't want. Both of you want the same goal (a sale). What is at issue is how and at what cost this is brought about.

THE AGREEMENT FORM

All estate agents must confirm their fees in writing, making it quite clear under which terms the fees become payable.

It is wise to ask to see an agreement form before giving instructions. Request a copy when you first visit an estate agent's office or once a valuation has been carried out.

Wherever possible avoid long contracts and do be sure that you can give a few days notice to terminate an agreement. Be wary, too, of the trap of having a clause in your agreement which allows the estate agent to earn a fee for a certain period of time after the agreement is terminated regardless of who actually sells the house. Finally, ask and agree in advance about what happens if you introduce the prospective purchaser yourself.

SOLE AGENCY OR MULTIPLE AGENCY?

Do you instruct one agent or several? The answer may partly depend on where you live – multiple agency is common in some parts of the country but not others.

Sole agency (instructing one agent only) *tends to be cheaper* and arguably creates the best professional relationship between a good agent and a vendor.

Normally (but read the agreement carefully), under sole agency you are not required to pay the commission if you sell the house yourself through, say, a personal contact.

A "sole selling agreement" could mean that you may not instruct other estate agents for some months; it may prevent you from selling privately, even to a relative, without incurring the estate agent's fee. Since a "sole agency agreement" tends to be more restrictive, an agent must spell out the meaning of the term clearly. (See *The Estate Agents (Provision of Information) Regulations 1991*, page 54)

The argument put forward against sole agency is that the agent may have too relaxed an attitude to a sale because he is not in competition with other estate agents. However, if the sole agency is only for a short term (say four weeks) the agent will still probably have every incentive to work hard for a sale.

Multiple Agency is where you instruct more than one agent and the whole commission is payable to whichever estate agent sells the house. The practice is most common in London and the South of England. Perhaps the main advantage of multiple agency is that competition among the estate agents in theory should increase the chances of a quick sale and a wider market being reached.

The drawbacks of multi agency include the fact that through your home appearing in a multiplicity of advertising pages it could give the impression that you may be desperate to sell. This erroneous impression could well attract potential buyers who are convinced that they can knock you down in price. Sometimes, too, confusion can arise as to just which estate agent has introduced a purchaser. You must therefore make sure that you are only going to pay one estate agent!

My own opinion is that sole agency on a no sale no charge basis, given to the *right* agent, will receive maximum attention and the best possibility of an early sale at the *least* cost. This is particularly true in a depressed market where a sole agent will naturally be more anxious to make any quick sales that he can.

THE OFFICES

Before instructing an estate agent or property shop, undertake an inspection of the local estate agency offices. Ask for some property details and have a chat with the staff. Professionalism

and enthusiasm are the two key ingredients to look for from the estate agency staff.

Having satisfied yourself on these points, what else should you look for? Many agents do not offer an efficient mailing list, but you want details of your home going to as many prospective purchasers as possible. Ask for the names and addresses of people who have received details of your house to be sent to you on a regular basis by the agent you decide to instruct.

Within this number there should be a hot list. This consists of people who can proceed to move immediately. Normally, they will be contacted by telephone by the estate agent. Staff enthusiasm is important here.

As part of the process of trying to achieve a quick sale the estate agent can, should you so desire, arrange to show people around your house whether you are there or not. Naturally you will want to feel complete confidence in the responsibility of the staff for this task.

Many estate agents create a window display by showing photographs of the houses on their books on rotating drums in their windows. At the time of giving your instruction negotiate with the estate agent to ensure that your house will always be featured in a favourable position in any such display. Surprisingly, very few people do make this request in my experience.

You will have gathered by now that the right promotion is crucial to a sale. This does not just apply to the offices. Always have a "for sale" board located in a prominent and easily visible position if at all possible.

NEGOTIATING ABILITY

Do you feel that the valuer and their staff are going to look after your best interests? Be aware of the rules of negotiation referred to elsewhere in this book.

A skilled negotiator is likely to get the highest possible price for you. He is in a stronger position to do this in booming times or where the prospective buyer is convinced that he has found his ideal house and is determined to have it.

Although your estate agent is your ally, you should not disclose to him the lowest price you would accept for your property. This advice applies even more strongly in the case of potential purchasers who are looking around – give no clues or indication to them.

Your agent's negotiating ability will also be important when prospective buyers have looked around and agreed to buy. Your agent must then check that the person wanting to go ahead is really in a position to do so.

My own opinion is that once a sale has been agreed you do not accept any higher offers. 'Gazumping' (effectively a betrayal of the intending buyer) has quite rightly become a dirty word. Imagine how you would feel if the vendor of the house you are buying cried off at the last minute unable to resist a higher bid.

INSIST THAT YOUR ESTATE AGENT KEEPS YOU FULLY INFORMED

It will of course not be possible to judge how well you will be kept informed by your chosen estate agent at the start. You could discuss how well an agent does in this respect if you have used him before or if you know someone else who has. Otherwise you will have to rely on making your requirements very clear.

It is important that you discuss with the estate agents exactly what kind of ongoing after service you will receive following their valuation. And don't just accept their word — ask them to put their promises in writing.

As matters get under way you will need to find out from your estate agent what impression the people who have viewed your home came away with. Specifically, the reasons they chose not to buy. If the people who looked around your property were impressed enough to want to buy it, you'll need the estate agent's advice on the merits of any offers that come forward and whether a reduction in price is necessary.

Once you have found a buyer it is crucial that both your estate agent and solicitor keep you fully informed of happenings over the weeks until contracts are exchanged. The estate agent will, of course, have to comply with the legislation. (See page 54)

THE VALUATION

Getting the valuation of your property correct is the key to successful selling. Pitch the price too low and you may sell quickly, but in so doing you could lose thousands of pounds. Pitch it too high and it may take a long time to sell, get stale on the market and mean a lower price has to be accepted in the end if a sale is to be achieved.

Much will depend, too, on the reasons underlying your sale. Ideally, you will be able to afford to sit tight until the right price is achieved. But you may have to move quickly (for instance to a new job elsewhere), in which case selling at a bargain price might be your only option.

What is required above all is that the price should be a realistic one. Always ask the valuer to justify how he has arrived at his figure. This should be seen within the context of similar properties in the area. Clearly, unless your property has special features (such as an extension) the figures should be quite alike. Obviously you will be very lucky to achieve a sale when cheaper alternatives are available, especially in a slow moving market.

Always wait to see what figure the valuer himself comes up with. Don't disclose the price you think is correct or what an alternative valuer has come up with until a decision is needed.

If there is one agent who you would prefer to use but whose valuation is slightly below that of another agent, never be afraid to telephone your preferred agent. Ask him if he would be prepared to take your house on at the higher figure. You can always come down in price; you can't go up. There is no such thing as a fixed price for a property. Most houses fall into price bands, plus or minus 10 to 15 per cent, around a central figure.

As indicated earlier, the time that you put your house on the market will be crucial to the level of profit you will realise on your property. The worst time to sell is during a period when house prices are falling because of poor demand.

WHICH QUALIFICATIONS?

The qualifications to look out for are the letters FRICS or ARICS, Fellow, or Associate, of the

Royal Institution of Chartered Surveyors and FSVA or ASVA, Fellow, or Associate, of the Society of Valuers and Auctioneers. To gain these qualifications involves high levels of academic achievement and the standards of professional ethics demanded are also high.

The other main estate agency qualifications to look out for are ANAEA or FNAEA – Associate, or Fellow, of the National Association of Estate Agents. This qualification is only available to experienced estate agents.

The benefits of experienced valuers are considerable. Apart from their professional integrity, they will probably be able to answer questions on building construction, essential repairs etc. with great authority and knowledge.

Above all else the valuer has to be keen and thorough and undertake a detailed inspection of your home both inside and out.

Professionalism and experience are vital. A property qualification is a great asset but does not necessarily make the individual a superb salesman. If the person valuing your home is a reasonably good salesman, satisfies the criteria on the checklist, *and* is qualified then you have potentially the best of both worlds.

SURVEY – HOW PEOPLE FIND THEIR HOMES

On a regular basis I carried out a survey of all people (buyers and sellers of property) with whom my estate agency dealt with, to determine how they came to find the house they were buying. It was surprising how the results from different offices were very similar. Below is a typical result taken across four offices.

In addition, it was established that 87 per cent of the 210 people surveyed were moving a distance of under 10 miles, with only 13 per cent relocating further afield.

Means of Finding Property	No.	Expressed as %
1. From visiting the office	52	25
2. First saw the 'For Sale' board	58	31
3. Estate agency advert	20	10
4. Heard from friends	8	4
5. From the mailing list	8	4
6. Not buying another/moving area	42	20
7. Other	12	6
TOTAL	210	100

This survey was carried out in the Midlands region and centred on the Coventry – Nuneaton area which is densely populated. The results were fairly consistent compared to similar surveys undertaken over different time periods.

What do the results mean to you? First, a for sale board, whether you are selling yourself or through an estate agent, is an essential. Almost a third of the houses sold in the survey were as a result of someone first seeing the board.

Second, the survey demonstrates how many people actually visited the estate agency offices. A quarter of sales were initiated from this point.

If we combine this section with those dealing with advertisements and mailing lists, they add up to 25 per cent plus 10 per cent plus 4 per cent, making a total of 39 per cent. This is a significant proportion of the whole and makes clear just how useful an estate agent can be in effecting a sale.

It is also interesting to note how many people move locally and not any great distance. Again, unless you have a property (such as a mansion) which will appeal to people outside your area, then a local estate agency should attract all your potential buyers by means of its activities.

RULES AND LAWS FOR ESTATE AGENTS

THE ESTATE AGENTS (PROVISION OF INFORMATION) REGULATIONS 1991

These far reaching regulations came into force on 29 July 1991. From that date all estate agents were obliged to give prospective clients a copy of their proposed terms in writing *before* taking instructions. If an agent is seeking sole selling rights or a sole agency then the P.I. regulations set out the wording for specific warning notices which must also be included.

The estate agent must also specify how his fee account will be structured and the commission and any expenses element must be fully particularised including VAT. The subsequent invoice should match the itemised estimate.

An estate agent also has to make it clear at what stage the "earning event" (entitlement to commission) becomes due. This normally occurs when the unconditional exchange of contracts takes place. But if, for example, it is to be at the stage of introducing a "ready, willing and able" buyer, then another statutory warning must be included.

It must also be made clear what, if anything, a seller will be charged if he takes his house off the market.

An estate agent must also make it clear to a seller if he is going to offer any services to a prospective buyer such as, say, a selling facility or financial services. If the prospective buyer decides to take advantage of such services the seller must be told both specifically and individually, although the legal obligation stops short of requiring the potential commission to be reported or disclosed. The obligation only runs until unconditional exchange of contracts. Thereafter the seller's position is settled and he cannot be further affected by the estate agent's actions.

The regulations also mention other "connected persons" such as a removal company whom the estate agent may recommend for gain to a prospective buyer. This information must be given in advance to the seller who theoretically, if so inclined, could withhold instructions to sell.

The regulations go even further. The Estate Agents (Undesirable Practices) Order 1991 requires *all* offers to be confirmed promptly and in writing, ideally the same day the offer is received. Details of offers should be given impartially and estate agents must not discriminate against buyers refusing any tie-in services, such as arranging mortgages through the agent, or give misleading information about prospective buyers.

The idea is to give the seller time to decide which offer to accept and prevent the agent guiding the client's judgement to the offer which will give the agent the greatest chance of any additional remuneration.

It would be an undesirable practice also for an estate agent not to disclose promptly and in writing if he or a close personal contact of his is interested in buying a property.

It would be an undesirable practice also for an estate agent to make a representation which is false with regard to matters such as room measurements, the tenure of property, proximity to services etc.

So what does all this mean to you? If you carefully read this section you will know what an estate agent is obliged to do in law. If for any reason the agent does not comply with the regulations referred to then you, as the seller, have no obligation to pay his fees and expenses without leave of a court. Should such a situation arise, you would be best advised to consult with your solicitor.

More importantly perhaps, by being aware just what a professional estate agent should be doing you can take some of the main points on board before you instruct your chosen estate agent.

You might even ask your chosen agent to confirm in writing that he is going to comply with all aspects of the Estate Agents (Provision of Information) Regulations and the Estate Agents (Undesirable Practices) Order 1991!!

OCEA

In 1990 the Ombudsman for Corporate Estate Agents Scheme was launched. The move provides further evidence of estate agents trying to raise their standards and improve their image. Most of the large estate agency groups are members and are bound by a Code of Practice. The terms specify that information given in sales particulars must not be misleading, there must be no compulsory tie-in of financial services, all offers must be confirmed in writing, etc.

This is, however, a voluntary code with no statutory backing. For complaints to be considered, consumers must first attempt to resolve the problem direct with the estate agent concerned. After this stage the Ombudsman can make substantial awards if he sees fit. Many claim an ombudsman scheme can only be successful if it has the full support of the industry it represents. Small independent estate agents are currently excluded from it, a

situation which will weaken OCEA as long as it prevails.

THE PROPERTY MISDESCRIPTIONS ACT 1991

The Act makes it a criminal offence to provide, without taking reasonable steps to verify the information, a false or misleading description of a property to a material degree. The Act sets out to extend the 1968 Trades Description Act to property.

The Act applies to residential and commercial estate agents, solicitors acting as estate agents, builders, developers and others engaged in the professional marketing of property. The PMA will be enforced by local authority trading standards officers. From October 1992 the statutory maximum fine on summary conviction is £5,000.

The main aim is to ensure that property is accurately described. In particular, statements must be based on fact not opinion, they need to be supported by evidence when reasonably possible; they should not be open to easily different interpretation and disclaimers will generally not be effective.

The Act offers one defence only – that of "due diligence". In order for this to succeed the defendant would have to prove "reasonable steps" had been taken to verify the accuracy of the particulars. It would be unwise for an estate agent to claim that a structural survey had been carried out on a house two years ago on the say so of a vendor. Sensible agents will seek written evidence.

What does all this mean to a house seller? It is important that a seller checks all the details given on his property very carefully indeed. It is possible that some agents will want a certificate from a seller to say that to the best of his belief and knowledge he has not given the estate agent false or questionable information.

THE ESTATE AGENCY CHECKLIST – POINTS TO CONSIDER WHEN CHOOSING AN ESTATE AGENT

1. Fees Quoted/No Sale No Charge

2. Agreement Form

3. The Offices

(a) Well located

(b) Smart efficient staff

(c) Clear window display

(d) Prompt phone response

(e) Mailing list operated

(f) Adverts well laid out

(g) Professional image

(h) Good property details

4. Negotiating ability

(a) Enthusiastic staff

(b) Will they look after your best interests?

(c) Ongoing customer care is good

5. The Valuation

(a) Experience, reputation and impression of valuer

(b) Professionalism and enthusiasm

(c) Valuer gives house a thorough inspection including outside

(d) Valuer has evidence to support his valuation and a very good knowledge of the area

ESTATE AGENTS: KEY MONEY MAKING AND SAVING POINTS

1. All estate agents are definitely not the same. Follow the guidelines on the estate agency checklist before choosing.

2. Try and negotiate on estate agency fees. At least shop around.

3. Do not sign any restrictive agreements. If in doubt let your solicitor see the estate agency agreement.

4. Always have a "for sale" board erected if possible.

5. Ensure that your house is advertised every week or fortnight and a special feature is placed on your behalf at no cost. Secure a prominent place in your agent's office/window.

6. Keep your house on the market and continue to let people view your house until all surveys and valuations are completed.

OTHER METHODS OF SALE

SELLING HOUSES BY AUCTION

The vast majority of houses are sold by private treaty. Such a method is generally cheaper than other methods (auction and tender).

Auction sales are often recommended where there is a legal requirement to satisfy beneficiaries, executors etc. A sale by auction is proof that every effort was made to obtain the best price. It is generally important that an auction is only recommended where one can expect to generate a lot of interest in a property. Hence in a buoyant housing market it may be ideal for a thatched country cottage or a house with land, but will not be suitable for a terraced or estate house.

If successful an auction has a final result. On the fall of the hammer the successful bidder is under contract to purchase in accordance with the terms and conditions set out in the auction details. A 10 per cent deposit has to be paid and completion will occur on a specified date – most often around 28 days later.

Auction sales are usually subject to an undisclosed reserve price and the auctioneer will normally reserve the right to bid on behalf of the vendor.

The disadvantages of auction sales are such that you should consider them carefully before choosing this method of sale. As public sales scheduled to take place on a certain date they can exclude some prospective purchasers who might otherwise have shown much interest. This applies especially to any people who need to sell their property to be able to buy and who do not want to resort to bridging finance. Another group who will be put off by a public auction comprises those who have not been able to complete their surveys, legal inquiries and the financial arrangements in time for the auction.

Another consideration is that auction sales and sale by tender are often more expensive than sale by private treaty as the legal documentation is more complex and all the additional selling costs are borne by the vendor.

When selling by auction you are likely to be responsible for the one off costs. Under this head will fall such extra items as additional room hire. However, there may still be some scope for negotiating the fee you are likely to be charged. Also bear in mind that relatively few estate agency firms can offer you a comprehensive auctioneering service and most auctioneers are professionally qualified.

The range of choice available will depend on your particular area. Where there are several firms able to undertake sales by auction you should judge them on the basis of the estate agency checklist. Additionally, you should consider what auctioneering experience the particular firm has, and the comments and advice of its auctioneer.

SELLING THROUGH PROPERTY SHOPS

There are variations on the types of property shops. For example, there are some that provide a virtually identical selling service to an estate agency either charging similar commission levels or slightly less; others are solicitor property shops giving an estate agency and legal conveyancing service often employing experienced estate agents; still others may be classified as "traditional" property shops in that they claim to give an estate agency service at a fraction of the cost.

As far as the different types of property shops are concerned, it is relatively easy to judge their performance by following the procedure outlined on the estate agency checklist. You will of course need to find out how the legal fees are charged by a solicitor property shop.

A large number of the "traditional" property shops failed within a very short space of time, the most notable example being Woolworth's property shop; others have become very well established in certain areas. If you are considering selling your house through a property shop it is still important to read the previous section about estate agents to compare what sort of service you are likely to receive.

Property shops often charge a set fee for limited press advertising. For any vendor who wants his or her property advertised regularly then the price may rise dramatically. So check this point.

For the set fee, a representative calls at a house, takes details, a photograph and erects a sales board. A newly registered property may appear for a period in the local press and might be shown in an individual property shop's own bulletin. Often an individual vendor decides the price. The property is displayed at the property "shop" (which is often an area of a large store).

Now let's compare property shops with estate agents. It is absolutely crucial that professional advice is taken on all aspects of the sale of your house. The importance of the right qualifications have already been stressed.

Essentially, accurate valuation calls for great professional skill. Too high a valuation will protract and stall the sale. Too low a figure could well lead to an immediate sale, but in the process hundreds and probably thousands of pounds will have been lost that could have been yours.

Thus, a person using a property shop may possibly save a few hundred pounds in agents' fees, but could lose many times more than this by underselling his property. Moreover, if you are going to undersell, could you perhaps do it yourself and save your fee?

Regular advertising with a property shop can take the cost up considerably – with no guarantee of a sale. Indeed, estate agents probably have a greater incentive to promote properties for sale because until they are off their hands they won't be paid.

Consider also that a lot of estate agents operate from shop fronts and are concentrated together. These provide a natural drawing point for anyone looking for property to buy. This observation also applies to those coming in from outside the area who may not know where to locate a property shop. In many cases, your property is unlikely even to be seen. Compared with a good estate agent, therefore, you are narrowing the range of buyers. And should you place your property with one of the larger estate agents then it may attract an even wider audience through its chain of shops dotted around the area.

In my experience estate agents are much better equipped to deal with the complications which often arise and need resolving before a sale can be completed. Let us suppose that a property is down-valued by the building society, or a retention is placed on the mortgage advance because big repairs are necessary (for instance, a new damp proof course or re-wiring). These factors can all cause a sale to "go off". Here the skilful estate agent can often manoeuvre so that the sale is not lost.

And what if you are faced with the situation of having sold your house but not yet being in a position, for whatever reason, to acquire another property? Some big estate agents who have large management departments are in a position to offer both vendors and purchasers rented accommodation should this become necessary.

KEY POINT

The major drawback with existing "traditional" property shops is that many require an up front payment that is not refundable. Indeed, you could well *lose* money rather than save it through taking this route.

Such "property shops" have a contract to advertise the house, not to sell it. Hence they have little interest in quick sales. They need a large stock to attract people to browse and thus encourage more sellers to buy space. As in most respects, you get what you pay for. Consider placing your property with a local estate agent if the property shop's terms don't suit you.

SELLING THE HOUSE YOURSELF

Finally, we come to the method of sale which could save you a considerable sum of money. You could be deluding yourself though. You might "save" up to £2,000 in agents fees, but end up selling your property for £5,000 less than you could have achieved through an estate agent. In such a case you *lose* money.

Saving estate agents' fees can also backfire on you. The prospective buyers, aware of this, could well insist on a substantial discount before agreeing to the sale. This will apply particularly in a slow moving market which will place you in a weaker position. If you are desperate to sell then you might have to agree.

The time you are most likely to achieve a good price is in a fast moving property market. So, unless circumstances force you to sell at another time, you will gain most financially through waiting for demand to pick up.

Valuation
It is strongly recommended that you should have several free valuations from estate agents. These won't cost you anything but will hopefully enable you to set a realistic price.

If an estate agent undertakes the valuation be prepared for him to advise you to let him manage the sale. Here you may say that you prefer to try to sell yourself, but will use his services in the event of failure.

The estate agent's visit can also serve another purpose. Before taking the plunge and opting for a self-sale route, ask yourself whether you are confident that you can provide as good a service as he does.

KEY POINT

To try and sell your own house will also cost money – possibly even several hundred pounds and with no guarantee of a sale. If you do the job properly, you will need a board, photographs of your house, particulars typed out, and a sum of money for advertising.

Be warned that you could fall flat on your face. During my career I have had occasion to visit houses which their owners had unsuccessfully tried to sell by themselves. Quite often, within a short space of time, my estate agency was able to arrange a successful sale.

As with selling anything else, presentation is important. This means that your own for sale board, particulars, photographs and adverts have to be very well presented indeed. And to achieve this you will have to spend money. It will also require quite a lot of time and effort, but the investment will be well worth it.

The Board

We have already seen how crucial a "for sale" board is. Unless there is a good reason, you just cannot do without one. It will stand as a free advert, attracting the attention of pedestrians and motorists and serving to "spread the word" that your house is on the market.

Professional presentation is the key. Simply to paint a board white and daub "for sale" over it will certainly save you money on the board but it won't help your

cause. You will stand confirmed as an amateur and prospective buyers will be put off. Far better to pay a carpenter to make the board and a professional sign writer to letter it for you.

By law the dimensions of the for sale board should not exceed 0.5 square metres. Furthermore, only one for sale board is allowed outside a property.

View your property as an enterprise seeking business. The sign will serve to attract customers. Ideally, your home should be available for viewing as much as possible. This could involve showing people round at odd hours, but if you are not able and ready to do this you are limiting your clientele.

On the other hand, your other commitments may prevent such an arrangement. In such an eventuality you can stop people calling round by inserting on the notice, "Viewing strictly by appointment", followed by a telephone contact number. This also has the advantage that you will be able to determine just when people are shown round. Another advantage is that you can convey further particulars over the phone to the prospective buyer. Having given these, if they are still interested then you may stand a better chance of a sale.

Once again, remember the security aspects mentioned earlier. You could always ask your caller for his name, address and phone number and say you will call him back to confirm a convenient time later. Again ask for the car registration number.

It may be that you are unable to have a board. In this case try having a window poster instead. Here again, though, consider the point that a professional printer will almost certainly do a much better job than you can.

Photographs
A photograph, or photographs, ought to be included in your advertisement. You can save money by taking the picture(s) yourself provided that you follow all the guidelines set out below.

View your house as a glamorous model which needs to be shown off in its best light. A full frontal view is usually the best. Always take photographs on a bright day to show off your home to best effect. Take several shots from different angles – even a whole film's worth. Then, when the pictures are developed, you will have a good selection to choose from just like a professional photographer with a model. Remember also that if one particular picture fails to work then you can always substitute another.

Property Details
Figures from the National Association of Estate Agents suggest that only 4 out of every 25 people taking the details of a property go on to view it. The main reason for having property details is that they are a sales aid if *correctly* presented. After someone has looked at a house they act as a reminder of what they have seen – rather like reading a newspaper to confirm what you have witnessed and heard on television. Another important point to remember here is that the measurements will be used for comparisons by the prospective buyers before they make their final choice. They might wonder, for instance, whether their existing carpets will fit certain rooms.

The key point to remember is to keep the particulars as straightforward and simple as possible, avoiding any confusing jargon or waffle. Stick to short sharp sentences on the whole and try to avoid flowery words like "delightful" and "charming".

It is equally important that prospective buyers are not deliberately misled especially in view of the ramifications of the Property Misdescriptions Act mentioned earlier. Although the Property Misdescriptions Act does not apply to individuals and private sales it is as well to stick to its spirit and remain accurate. Superlatives are only likely to arouse suspicions. Always use a disclaimer similar to the one shown in the example below. On the other hand, always bring out the good points of your home – for example, if you have recently had an expensive kitchen fitted or a new bathroom suite installed then emphasise this.

In providing particulars to prospective buyers who have been tempted to look further, you should set them out as follows.

Note that from January 1995 it will be necessary to put metric measurements first on property details, in letters no smaller than the imperial measurements.

6 EARLS ROAD, ANYTOWN

DESCRIPTION AND LOCATION

The property is situated in one of the town's popular locations affording easy daily access into Anytown town centre with its many shops, offices and schools. It is also within easy reach of all local business centres.

ACCOMMODATION

Pillared Entrance Porch With hardwood front entrance door.

Entrance Hall Having central heating radiator, telephone point, central heating thermostat control, understairs cupboard and stairs off.

Lounge 16'8" × 11'4". Having an attractive Natural Stone fireplace with fitted gas fire, tv aerial point, central heating radiator.

Dining/Kitchen 17'8" × 8'5". With excellent range of fitted base units, draws and matching eye level storage cupboards, inset sink unit with single drainer and mixer tap, breakfast bar; superbly refurbished 6 months ago, central heating radiator, French doors leading to the lounge.

First Floor Landing Having 2 built-in cupboards.

Bedroom 1 (rear) 11'7" MAX × 11'. Having built-in wardrobe cupboard housing the lagged copper cylinder, central heating radiator.

Double Bedroom 2 (front) 10' MAX × 6'10". Having central heating radiator.

Bedroom 3 (front) 8'6" × 6'10". Having central heating radiator.

Fully Fitted Bathroom Having suite in Avocado comprising: a panelled bath with Triton T80 shower and shower screen, pedestal wash hand basin, low flush w.c., central heating radiator, artexed ceiling.

ADDITIONAL FEATURES

Outside The property has gardens to 3 sides, the front garden being mainly lawned with flower and shrub borders. There is a tarmacadamed driveway, providing parking for two vehicles, leading to the Brick Built Garage, 18' × 8'6". There is a brick built wall with timber gate leading to the side garden which is lawned with a variety of flowers and shrubs. Enclosed Rear Garden which has a concrete slabbed patio area. The remainder is laid to lawn with further flowers, shrubs and trees.

ADDITIONAL INFORMATION

Tenure Freehold

Services All main services are connected to the property. Full gas central heating and double glazing.

Viewing Arrangements To view telephone 123456.

PRICE £74,000

*These details are set out as a general guide only and do not form part of any contract. All descriptions and dimensions are given in good faith and are believed to be correct.

Advertising

We have seen earlier that people most often only move locally. This makes it imperative that you advertise in the local newspaper. The day to choose would be the same day of the week chosen by estate agents and property shops in the vicinity to promote the property they have on their books. Prospective buyers will purchase this edition of the newspaper and comb through it in search of properties to suit their tastes and spending budget. You will therefore attract your biggest audience by advertising on this particular day.

On the other hand, there is an equally valid argument in favour of advertising on a different date, say on a Friday or Saturday, when circulation also tends to be higher than normal. Because there will be so few properties in the advertising section – indeed yours might even be the only example – your house is bound to stand out and be noticed more. To be sure of this, buy a larger than usual space. Even if this does cost you that little bit extra, your trouble could well pay big dividends.

It is important to be clear about what your advertisement is going to cost you. Remember that you may well have to advertise several times before you are successful. Where more than one newspaper is published locally, I would suggest that you first establish the respective costs of each since these tend to vary. You can then draw up an advertising budget.

You cannot be certain at the outset how much your advertising will cost you. Obviously if you achieve a quick sale your outgoings in this respect will be considerably less than if it takes some time to offload your home onto a buyer.

In the latter eventuality, be prepared to change your

advertising strategy. You could switch from one publication to another, change the day on which the advert appears, and switch the photograph.

There are two types of advert: display and classified.

Display adverts are promotions placed among other boxed adverts. As such they are bound to attract the reader because of their collective impact.

Classified adverts will appear in a particular advertising column of the newspaper – probably "Property for Sale". You could save yourself expense here by restricting your advert to the briefest description and by avoiding the use of a photograph. However, my advice would be not to spare any expense especially in the first stages of your advertising campaign. A bolder and bigger than usual advert with a photograph serves as a natural focal point beside which other property adverts tend to get lost.

Having made this point, remember that the very fact that you are advertising ought to generate some interest even if you choose the sparsest of adverts to promote your cause. People wishing to buy a home will often comb through the property section in meticulous detail.

What is crucial is that you say enough to make potential buyers want to find out more. Pick out the key *benefits* that your home has. At the same time you need to give the advert a punchy headline that will stand out. For instance, you might start with "10 Blackers Close, Anytown. Must sell, absolute bargain." Provided that your price matches this introduction you ought to attract considerable interest.

What you must do is avoid jargon and verbosity. Simple adverts are best. And don't overstate your case. Your photograph will say much more than words can, so always ensure that the one selected does full justice to the property. Otherwise, it is pointless to use one.

Pack as much information as possible into your advert. You can achieve this by avoiding repetition. For instance, you would be repeating yourself to state "This is a low price and represents very good value for money."

Make a point also of asking prospective buyers what they thought of the advert. In particular, you need to know whether they felt that your home matched the expectations generated by the advert. If it doesn't then you need to rework your advert.

I have prepared an advert on the property mentioned earlier. This is the type of short, sharp promotion that you could consider using.

PRICED FOR QUICK SALE!

Photograph

6 Earls Road Anytown

Very well presented semi. Many excellent features including double glazing and recently re-furbished kitchen. Hall, lounge, dining/kitchen, 3 bedrooms, bathroom including shower. Large garden. To view telephone 123456.

OTHER METHODS OF SALE: KEY MONEY MAKING AND SAVING POINTS

1. Consider selling by auction only if your house has unusual features and will thereby attract plenty of bids. On the other hand, if your home is nothing out of the ordinary choose another method of sale.

2. Not all property shops are the same. Find out what you will be charged before agreeing to selling through one of them.

3. Try and negotiate a fee reduction if you opt to sell through a property shop.

4. If you decide to sell yourself go over the previous section carefully. Ensure your valuation is correct.

5. Have an estate agent in mind should your efforts at self-selling prove unsuccessful.

6. Be very careful you do not under sell by selling yourself. Remember, also, that a prospective buyer will know you are not incurring estate agency fees and may expect a reduction in price.

7. If you sell yourself, pay particular attention to professional presentation. It is absolutely crucial.

SECTION 4: PRESENTING AND MAINTAINING YOUR HOME TO SELL IT

PRESENTATION

THE PRIME IMPORTANCE OF PRESENTATION

The presentation of a house for sale is crucial. Not only can it determine whether a sale is achieved, it can also make several thousand pounds difference to the final price.

My definition of presentation in this context would be how well a house looks both internally and externally, how attractive the garden is, how welcoming the house is (creating a warm and cosy feeling is most important), the decorative state, and the standard of furnishings, including curtains and carpets.

Because in my experience up to 10 per cent of your price can be down to the presentation it is important that we look at the subject in some depth. You only have to consider the great lengths to which builders go to generate sales for new houses. Show-houses cost many thousands of pounds to present and to staff yet their availability is deemed to be essential by many builders.

In a sense, you need to view your own home in the same light as a showhouse. Of course, it is unlikely that you will be able to afford to redecorate and refurnish to any great extent, but there are a lot of things you can do without involving too much trouble and expense.

FIRST IMPRESSIONS ARE CRUCIAL

"You never get a second chance to make a first impression." This saying may seem trite, but it is especially true when it comes to selling houses – first impressions are lasting impressions. I have spoken to many people who have said that within minutes of walking into a house they knew instinctively that it felt "right" and from this feeling followed a desire to buy. Equally, if the right atmosphere and presentation are missing so the prospective buyers will rapidly conclude that your house is not for them.

Basically, your house should be as clean, tidy and uncluttered as possible. Remember that you are trying to sell a lifestyle. If

your house is in a chaotic state then you stand very little chance of selling it unless your price reflects this chaos. But with the right preparation for a sale you can not only achieve a successful sale but also stand to "make" a considerable sum through a good selling price.

EXTERNALLY

First, ensure that the garden is looking good. This won't be easy if you are looking for a winter sale, but in the summer months ensure that lawns are neatly mowed with meticulously cut edges. A good spread of flowers, presenting an array of colours also helps to create the right impression. Expenditure on flowers and decorative plants won't necessarily cost the earth.

By the same token, don't be afraid to take out trees or shrubs which obscure views. What you are looking for is to create a feeling of space. Trees should be planted on the boundary of the property. Conifers are always a top favourite, but if you employ these do go for different shapes and colours to create a visually interesting effect. The same is true for shrubs.

Bear in mind, too, that gardens need maintaining. Not all of your potential buyers are going to be keen gardeners and could well be put off by the thought of a lot of gardening work. Such buyers tend to prefer a simple garden where a lawn takes up most of the ground, with a slabbed path running up it to the house. Large lawns also help to add to the feeling of space. Try to keep flower beds to a reasonable size.

Unless the privacy of your house requires a thick front hedge, consider either removing it altogether or at least cutting it down to let in more light. And don't forget the front gate – if it's rotten, replace it, if it creaks oil it, if it needs a new coat of paint see to this. With larger houses, look out for a grander entrance – nothing is more impressive to the visitor than a well designed entrance.

Next, ask yourself whether the exterior of your property is looking good. This means no peeling doors or window frames or dirty door steps. Ensure the windows sparkle both outside and in. Any moving slates, broken or missing tiles, cracked window panes and anything else which is in a less than perfect state should be remedied.

But think twice before going further than this. Major alterations won't necessarily make your house more sellable and could well have the opposite effect.

Too many sellers don't bother about garages – but be assured that buyers, most of whom will be car owners, will give them a good looking over. Unless your garage is a large one, or you own a small car, a good tip is to leave your vehicle outside the garage. This will make it appear bigger than it actually is. Ensure that any oil stains have been removed, remove all rubbish and make sure everything is tidy. Allow the buyer the try his car for size if he wishes.

INTERNALLY

When choosing a colour scheme try to keep to pale neutrals as these help to make a house look more spacious and are restful on the eye. To move away from neutral colours only risks offending the buyer who will be put off by the thought of having to redecorate to suit his tastes. Full redecoration is not called for, but do repair peeling wallpaper and damaged paintwork.

All small DIY jobs should be attended to by replacing broken door knobs, sash cords etc. Ensure, though, that any work on DIY lines isn't botched – amateurish repair work will stand out a mile. All light bulbs and electrical appliances should be in full working order.

SPACIOUSNESS

Make your home as spacious as possible. For instance, you might spread clothes out in wardrobes, leaving one or two empty coathangers. Get rid of all the unnecessary rubbish and clutter. Invest in some mirrors to make rooms look bigger. This applies especially to bathrooms and to the ends of corridors.

Bathrooms and kitchens are crucial rooms and can sell houses by themselves if presented well. A really well equipped and sparklingly clean kitchen will help to bring about a sale. So too will a homely and alluring bathroom. New or recently cleaned curtains in a bathroom help to bring about this effect. In both rooms place a few plants. When you have prospective buyers coming to view your home, make quite sure that the kitchen and bathroom are really tidy. Get rid of all soggy towels and dirty plates!

In winter ensure that your home is warm and comfortable. Turn up the central heating to a reasonable level or, where applicable, ensure that a glowing fire has been lit some time before the visit takes place.

DO NOT FORGET THE UNDERRATED SENSE OF SMELL

Creating the right "feeling" also means eliminating all smells which might be offensive. Be careful to get rid of such smells – stale tobacco in the atmosphere of rooms can be very offputting (keep all ashtrays empty), so too can be animal smells, or foods, such as garlic. Take care not to cook before an appointment with a prospective buyer.

If possible, have a pot of filter coffee available. Also have plenty of fresh flowers such as freesias around your home which give off a pleasant and natural odour. Also ensure that the house is well aired.

For cloakrooms and bathrooms pot-pourri and scented soap are very effective. You can buy small bottles of revitalizer from shops.

A particularly good idea is to have one of the brass rings that fit over lamp bulbs to give off a very alluring smell. The smell of polish and a soft cleansing agent in kitchens can be very effective.

PRESENTATION: KEY POINTS

1. Presentation of your home is crucial to selling it at the maximum possible price within the shortest possible time. Up to around 10 per cent of the price you achieve can depend on how well your home is presented.

2. Always take a look at new showhouses to give you ideas on the ideal way a home should look.

3. A spotless kitchen and bathroom are perhaps the two key rooms.

KEEP YOUR HOME WELL MAINTAINED

We have seen the importance of presentation in selling houses at the maximum price in the shortest possible time. Closely connected to this is how well a house is maintained. Prospective buyers are likely to try to negotiate lower prices for what they feel are items of disrepair especially when a surveyor alerts them to the fact.

Remember that even if you are good at DIY and intend to do the work which may be necessary yourself, it must invariably be done to professional standards. Otherwise, while you might save money on maintenance the end result can only be to devalue your house, creating an opening for the buyer to seek to knock the price down.

There are several DIY books on the market which are good guides on particular aspects of home maintenance. Many can be found in DIY stores.

Accompanying the DIY boom, hire shops have sprung up all over the country. From these you can hire out all manner of DIY tools. The cost isn't cheap and you'll normally be charged either an hourly or a daily rate. Against this, the quality of the tools can save you much time and effort.

Let's talk specifics. The main items to bear in mind are as follows.

EXTERNAL DECORATION

Doors and windows need to look well maintained. They will be made of wood, metal or plastic, or a combination of these. Problems will arise as a result of old age or where the repainting is neglected. Whatever material is used for doors and windows, moisture will affect them from the outside and condensation from the inside.

Check the bottom halves of doors (including garage doors) to see that they are not affected by dampness.

Steel casement windows are susceptible to corrosion, especially if they date from the 1930's when steel did not benefit from a galvanised protective coating. Eventually corrosion will cause windows to crack and hinges and window catches to break. Aluminium and plastic frames, a modern development, don't have this problem.

Your house will probably need redecorating externally every four years or so because of exposure to the vagaries of the British climate.

You should seriously consider having the exterior of your house redecorated if necessary before putting it on the market. Go for neutral colours (white is best) and ones which are in keeping with the surrounding properties. There is a good chance that you will recoup much of your costs. Eccentric colour schemes look garish and will put off all but the most eccentric buyer.

ROOFS

If you have any missing tiles or slates on your roof they should be replaced as soon as possible. Not doing so will only invite damp to penetrate into the building (leading ultimately to problems with internal ceilings) while the wind will take off more tiles from the affected area.

Roofs are either pitched or flat. In the past pitched roofs were covered with slates, clay tiles, stone tiles, wooden shingles or thatch. Today the commonest practice is to cover pitched roofs with concrete tiles.

Be careful with flat roofs. Many in houses are felted roofs (often on garages) and many have a life of around fifteen years – often less. Failure to refelt at this point will compound the ensuing problems. Any indication of water penetrating a flat roof calls for urgent attention.

CHIMNEY

Should there be dampness on the chimney breast the usual cause will either be ineffective brickwork in the chimney stack above roof level, or poor sealing between chimney and roof –

usually defective lead flashing or cracked cement fillets. Make sure your chimney is well pointed and that the lead flashing (where the chimney meets the roof) is in good repair.

Apparent "dampness" can occur in older properties as a consequence of gases from a solid fuel boiler or grate mixing with the moisture at the top of the flue, where it is cooler, to form acids which eat into the brickwork, mortar and plaster. Where this has happened, the remedy lies in stripping away all the contaminated plaster, cleaning the exposed brickwork to remove any lurking salts, then applying a sealer to the brickwork and replastering with a sand and cement backing coat and Sirapite finish.

GUTTERS AND DOWNPIPES

Most gutters are made from either cast iron, zinc, asbestos, cement or plastic. They will be connected to downpipes which could well be made of the same materials, though the common practice today is to renew these with the plastic variety, so it is now quite normal for cast iron gutters to feed into plastic piping. Where you need to replace any piping, go for the plastic type – it is much easier to fit and can be cut easily.

Whatever the material involved, a lack of maintenance

can result in problems building up. For instance, failing to protect cast iron gutters through regular painting will bring on rust. Any blockages are full of potential problems – in winter when water freezes burst pipes will be the outcome.

Often the causes of blockages are either leaves or silt finding their way into the gutters and downpipes. Once there they must be removed. Prevention is better than cure here. Adding wire or plastic balloons in the gutter outlets can save you a lot of hassle. It is important to keep gutters and downpipes clear at all times. Ensure leaves and other debris are cleared out and that there are no leaks. Otherwise, problems can occur with water falling onto and penetrating brickwork.

EXTERNAL WALLS

A common task that often needs doing is the repointing of any perished mortar. If this is not done then water can easily penetrate the walls and cause dampness inside the building.

If your house is rendered or pebble dashed make sure that these are in good condition. Where the rendering has cracked or bulges out, you will need to hack it off and replace it.

New brickwork can sometimes cause a problem when a white powder appears, causing surface discoloration (efflorescence). It will go away in time, but you will need to hose the wall down thoroughly for the brickwork to be seen to best advantage by potential buyers.

INTERNALLY

Keep on top of decoration (neutral colours, remember), repair items like light bulbs and leaking taps, dealing with them as soon as possible. Otherwise, internal maintenance problems will accumulate.

One of the finest investments you as a homeowner can make is a regular programme of maintenance. Prevention is better than cure. For example, it is far, far better to paint window sills regularly than replace rotten wood every five or six years. Bear in mind that no matter how many features are added to a house its value will fall if normal basic maintenance is not carried out.

AND MY DAD WORKS IN THE
PLANNING OFFICE ...

SECTION 5:
EXTENSIONS AND
IMPROVEMENTS

This sections looks at:

EXTENSIONS

If you are thinking of extending your house bear in mind that what adds value to it varies according to its type and location. Virtually any house has a ceiling price tag based on its situation, which will remain fixed irrespective of the nature and extent of extensions.

Any extensions must be well designed and fit with the existing building. Where major extensions or costly improvements are involved it is worth taking advice from a chartered surveyor or architect before proceeding.

It is important to check on planning permission before you start to build. If a terraced house is not being enlarged beyond 10 per cent of the original building or a semi detached or detached by more than 15 per cent then extensions will usually be approved by the planning authority. However, where a listed building is involved then planning permission will be needed.

In any event, all work will have to comply with building regulations. Talk all this through with either the surveyor or a reputable building contractor. You should also consider asking for several estimates from some respected builders. Be careful to avoid the cowboy variety – they will only be cheaper in the short term. There are a few telltale signs which will help you identify this type – no receipts, a demand for an up-front cash payment, cheaper quotes in return for cash payments to avoid tax, and a reluctance to put anything in writing.

You must be clear in your own mind as to exactly what kind of improvement you require. Then either prepare a specification of the work yourself or have it done professionally. That way you can ensure that all the firms you approach are quoting for the same job. You should select at least three firms to give written estimates so that you can get a reasonable cross sample. It is best to choose firms which belong to a trade association.

Whatever firm is involved, large or small, professional or cowboy, there is always the risk that they will go bankrupt before the extension is complete. The Federation of Master Builders operates a guarantee scheme to cover this contingency and which will also protect homeowners against poor workmanship. If you want this guarantee, you will have to pay a sum in advance to the F.M.B. Of course, this will increase your costs, but you have the comfort of insuring yourself against the worst eventualities.

Extensions can take the form of single-storey extensions, extensions over a garage, or even two storey extensions. Whatever type of extension, be careful to ensure that the cost involved will not push the overall value of your home way over the ceiling price for your area.

The key point to remember is that the new extension has to be tasteful and in keeping with the house and the surrounding area. Otherwise it will stand out like a sore thumb and become a distraction rather than an attraction.

Be careful, too, that you do not use up too much garden space.

You are likely to recoup over 50 per cent of the cost of a tasteful extension, always provided that the location of your property warrants the resulting price.

DO IMPROVEMENTS ADD VALUE TO YOUR HOME?

Much depends on the region as to which improvements have more value. In Scotland and the North, where the winter weather can be biting, double glazing is more highly valued than elsewhere. The South East has the highest proportion of DIY improvements (here 1 in 5 indulge in home improvements for a hobby); in the East, extensions are very popular, as are fitted kitchens. The South West, South Wales and the Midlands are the areas where gardening is most popular (so a patio wouldn't go unappreciated), but in Greater London, where most gardens are small, work outside the house won't generally be a big selling feature.

Every year, Britain's inhabitants engage in home improvements, but very few of them are aware of the implications as far as their house value is concerned, often blithely assuming that any alteration adds value to a property. In fact, with very few exceptions you are wasting money in improving your home if you intend to move within two or three years. A great many people move house after five years whether or not that is their intention at the start of the period.

It is important, therefore, that generally you conceive house improvements as being for your own benefit, although I will try and give some indication of what sort of costs you can expect to recoup from improvements should you decide to move. Bear in mind that improvements are different from general maintenance. You must carry out the latter if you are to maximise the price you sell your house for.

There are two golden rules. First, not all improvements are beneficial. Some improvements can actually reduce the value of your house and not increase it! Second, improvement work should be done to professional standards or not at all.

Keep any alterations balanced. For example, if an en suite bathroom can only be installed by halving the size of the next biggest bedroom in a four bedroom house then the probability is that you will be shooting yourself in the foot. It may be impossible for the affected room to serve as a bedroom any longer and even if it can be a bedroom prospective buyers will almost certainly be put off by its reduced proportions. Similarly, adding a fourth bedroom to a three bedroom house may not be wise where the alternative would be to add another reception room. Above all, ensure that any changes are in character with the rest of the house.

If you live in a listed building you will need the consent of your local authority before embarking on any improvements or major repair work. There are a number of publications now available which will help. Details may also be available from the local authority.

DO NOT OVER IMPROVE

Many people are under the very mistaken illusion that the more they spend on improvements to their house the more will its value increase. They are then quite shocked when an estate agent values their house for a much lower figure than they had expected.

Sure, a few strategic improvements will give your property the edge over similar properties in your vicinity, but be careful not to go overboard. The plain fact is that there is a maximum price for a given type of house in a particular area. The best, or most improved, house is virtually always held down in value by cheaper properties around it. If you are thinking of extensive improvements and extensions it will probably be more beneficial to move house.

CASE STUDY

One case stands out in my mind of a house which was over improved.

It was situated in a much sought after location, but still its facilities were way above the norm for the area.

"Improvements" in the early 1980's included a large heated swimming pool which cost over £30,000 then, a hard tennis court, taking up well over half of the original garden, a very expensive top-of-the-range German kitchen, and a white log cabin with sauna. Definitely not the features that you would ex-

pect to find in the location. In fact they wouldn't be out of place in millionaire's row! The normal ceiling figure for the area was around £100,000. The property sold for £6,000 above that figure, but only after it had spent several months on the market. It would have perhaps made only a few thousand pounds less than this without nearly £50,000 being spent on it. The owner even admitted that he had over improved, but said that he had enjoyed the facilities and at the time of making them never thought he would be moving.

There are numerous other examples of people not expecting to move and making improvements without a view to selling. They have come to realise their mistake too late.

WORTHWHILE IMPROVEMENTS

Generally speaking, worthwhile improvements fall into two categories: those that add value to your home; and those which, while probably not adding value, could assist you in selling your home.

In the early 1990's the Halifax Building Society published a major report on home improvements and DIY. It revealed that over half of all men and a quarter of all the women surveyed were engaged in modernising and improving their homes as opposed to simple maintenance.

During the 1980's a third of all owner occupiers chose to install double glazing, 35 per cent opted for a new kitchen, 24 per cent a new bathroom and 20 per cent central heating. Below, I will consider the improvements which are "good" and worthwhile.

KITCHEN

A well fitted kitchen is perhaps the most important requirement to sell a house. Over recent years it has taken on the form not just of a cooking and eating area, but also one where family and friends can be entertained. Where a couple are looking to buy your home and you really impress the woman with the kitchen layout then you are well on the way to a sale.

If you want to attain maximum saleability try to choose a "neutral" type of kitchen. Keep in mind a plain colour scheme with a light wood. For example, a pine or light oak kitchen will not date as quickly if chosen with care. Some modern kitchens can look out of date very quickly. Generally, the more modern the kitchen appliances that are available the more appealing will this room be. Where possible, it is best to locate your washing machine and tumble drier in a nearby "utility" room.

BATHROOMS

The bathroom is another very popular room and therefore it pays to improve it where needed. For example, if your bathroom dates from the immediate post-war decades (1950's– 1960's) it may be well worth your while to tear it apart and thoroughly modernise. Try and use natural or pastel colours for your bathroom suite and tiling. And remember to be consistent – do not have a brass towel rail and chrome taps.

At the upper end of the market, a bathroom or shower room en suite to the master bedroom is very important indeed. For this reason, you will find that the bathroom conversion business is a very competitive one so ask for several quotes.

The increase in value will be determined by how poor the state of the old bathroom was.

CENTRAL HEATING

Improving your central heating is probably the best move you can make. Prospective house buyers are now becoming very discerning and a good, efficient central heating system is now almost an essential requirement. Without a central heating system you will find it extremely difficult to sell your home and your asking price would need to reflect this major omission.

You might even be asked to produce bills to back up any claims that yours is a cost effective system. *A warming thought is that you should recover most of your expenditure here.*

GARAGES

A garage is essential for any quality house or where parking is at a premium. If you have the space, a double width garage is better than a double length one because then the cars can be removed without difficulty. Avoid cheap looking garages. The right garage can put your house into a higher price bracket especially in cities where parking is at a premium and cars parked on the road are vulnerable to theft and vandalism.

CONSERVATORY

Conservatories have become very fashionable over recent years and can add useful space to your house. To add value though, you must go for quality. A conservatory adds a new dimension to your garden, and to summer evenings. Make sure though that the conservatory will have the right aspect and view. *You should stand to take back over half of your costs.*

DOUBLE GLAZING

This is one of the most popular home improvements of all and does have the benefit of better heat and sound insulation. These features are particularly important where a property is exposed to high winds or is situated near a busy road. Be careful, though, to ensure that the double glazing windows fit the style of your house. As an investment double glazing is not so attractive – *you are likely to recover less than half of your outlay*, but your own comfort will be increased in the time that you remain in the home.

AVOIDABLE IMPROVEMENTS

There are several improvements which won't readily help you to sell your home and where you will not recover the costs involved.

SWIMMING POOLS

A contentious home improvement and one which is difficult to assess in terms of added value. For families with young children pools can be a dangerous hazard for obvious reasons. Pools were more popular some years ago, but their drawbacks have become all too plain – they are expensive to clean, heat and maintain. Outdoor pools are usually best avoided because of their limited use. Nonetheless, at the top end of the market they might perhaps be a worthwhile addition.

GAMES ROOM

Where you are selling to a couple with a young family, a games room represents an added attraction. Again, it is not easy to judge the amount of value such a feature would add, though you could look to save some money by converting a spare bedroom rather than having an extension built. The latter would be a necessity were a full size snooker table to be built. Snooker is now the most popular sport activity in Britain and so such a room would be a definite selling point. At the same time, it is not essential and probably won't be the decisive factor in achieving a sale or not.

LANDSCAPING AND TERRACING

These will add little if anything to the value of your house, though they may well be a strong selling feature. Unless your garden is a large one, a general tidying up and weeding should be enough.

It could be that you have spent money on making improvements everywhere else, but have failed to take your garden into account. Where the garden is large you might consider having it landscaped. If you decide on this course, don't employ cowboys with just a barrow and spade. Look instead to employ a reputable landscaping firm.

Your first step will be to contact the British Association of Landscape Industries (See page 92 for address). It has 700 members in Britain whose services are thoroughly vetted. BALI also acts when mediation is required.

Obviously costs vary according to the nature and size of the job. Walls, fences, paving, designing and planting – these are just some of your options. A good landscaping firm will first survey your garden and then propose several options with differing costs.

Remember, too, that landscaping takes time to have effect. Indeed, you might need to wait eighteen months or more for the full impact of your redesigned garden, until shrubs, trees, bushes and other plants, begin to fulfil their role.

Where a small garden is involved, be careful not to overdo it. Too many plants, trees, shrubs and flowers can create a cluttered effect and possibly obscure views from the house.

LOFT CONVERSIONS

In many modern houses with roof trusses close together it is not possible to convert the roof space. Another problem is that if you want the convenience of stair access a stair case can take up a lot of space and have the effect of making your house look cramped, a definite turn-off.

If you are not very careful, a loft conversion will only be of limited use. Because of a loft's proximity to the roof, it will need to be heated and insulated, often an expensive process. But while this is an essential requirement for winter access it makes lofts uncomfortably hot during the summer when many houses are sold.

At the same time, if there is no room to extend elsewhere, a loft conversion can create more space and, carried out in the right way, it may be a feature which I would recommend provided that there is sufficient room to place stairs (alternatively you might go for fold-up stairs). You can expect to recover over half the costs.

GRANNY FLATS

As their name suggests, granny flats are designed to accommodate elderly relatives within a home. Their appeal will vary according to the prospective buyer. What is probable, though, is that a fair proportion of potential buyers could be put off by this feature – we all know some jokes about the mother-in-law! Unless family reasons dictate that you have to incorporate a granny flat, then you'd probably be wise to avoid this improvement.

HOW TO SELL A DILAPIDATED HOME

The opposite extreme to a new house is one in a dilapidated condition. Yet you may come into possession of such a property, whether by accident or design, and with the correct degree of renovation you can stand to make a handsome profit.

Inheriting a poorly maintained house is commonplace where a close relative dies. Alternatively you might have lived abroad for some time and return to find your old home in a run down condition. Or you may have bought a house specifically to renovate it. In short, there are all manner of situations in which you can come to confront a house in dire need of repair.

In this type of situation, before doing anything to the house, consider having several valuations and use them as the basis for discussion with an experienced estate agent. If the property needs a lot of work doing to it – for instance, a new damp proof course, new floors and windows – the cost of restoration may be so prohibitive as to persuade you that the best course is to sell the property now, in its present condition.

At the same time, the lack of renovation may itself be a factor in preventing a sale to genuine potential buyers because it causes mortgage problems. It is likely that you will be able to sell to a builder, but only at a very knock-down price. They, like you if you were to choose the renovation route, naturally want to maximise their profit margins.

HOW CAN YOU MAKE MONEY IN BUYING, IMPROVING AND SELLING A HOUSE?

The mechanics of doing this are fairly straightforward. First you have to buy the property to be improved for the lowest price you can. Part of the secret of success is buying the right property at the right price in the first place. The property has to be in an area where, once it is done up, it is easily saleable at a significantly higher figure.

Secondly, you need to know what work to do to the property to bring it up to the standard to sell it; you need to know the cost of undertaking this work. Prices can vary so if you are employing a builder be sure to have several quotations.

Thirdly, you have to be able to fund the purchase price and the cost of improvement of the work prior to selling it.

Fourthly, you have to pay all professional and legal costs including possible stamp duty on your purchase, legal fees on both purchase and sale, estate agents and possibly architects fees if any extension work is necessary.

Finally, you have to be able to sell the house at a sufficiently high figure for the exercise to be worthwhile. This is shown very simply in the example below.

Old house bought for	£28,000
Cost of work to bring it up to required standard	£10,000
Legal fees on sale and purchase	£600
Estate agents fee	£750
Bank interest fees	£1,000
Selling price	£50,000
Profit	£9,650

On the face of it a straightforward exercise, but you need to be clear about certain objectives. First, are you going to be able to sell the house for a good price? It may not make sense doing the exercise in deteriorating areas where properties are falling in price, so make sure that you research the market. As well as the general conditions in the property market, be aware of the type of buyer of your property is liable to appeal to. A tastefully improved terraced house could well appeal to a first-time buyer but might not appeal to second or third time buyers looking to move up.

Second, are the properties with improvement potential readily available? In the 1980's many people jumped on the house improving bandwagon and there may be well be an acute shortage of improvable opportunies in your area. If so you are liable to face competition for houses which will push up the price.

Sometimes builders "buy" work to keep them ticking over so there may be competition from this direction.

Third, when improving it is important to know how far to go with "improvements" whilst at the same time making the property saleable.

Finally, be prepared for the house to take longer to sell than you hoped. If you intend to live there yourself for a period there may not be a problem because then you can decide when to place your home on the market.

In my experience, very many builders and property renovators make the mistake of putting their creation on the market before it is completed. Yet this is not a good idea, especially in the early stages of building. Of course, should you attract a buyer at this stage then it will give you an incentive to finish, but you're also likely to find many would-be buyers put off by the ongoing building which can be messy. Whether buying a new house or a refurbished one, most people prefer to see it fully finished before committing themselves to a purchase.

TAX QUESTIONS

The key point to bear in mind is that if you sell a house that is not your main residence then you will be liable to taxation.

You will either pay Capital Gains Tax or income tax. Capital Gains Tax is levied on gains in any one year over and above the tax free limit that is set by the Chancellor.

If you buy and sell several properties quickly and often, you will be treated as a property dealer by the Inland Revenue, and you will be liable to pay income tax on the profits of sales.

HOUSE RENOVATION GRANTS

In 1990 major changes took place regarding house renovation grants. The new grants system is clearly explained in a brochure published by the Department of the Environment and available from your local council.

It is advisable to visit the latter to discuss any grant matters with the appropriate officials.

The type of grant most appropriate is the renovation grant which covers the improvement or repair of dwellings. It is important to bear in mind that the property for which you are making the application must be either your only or your main residence.

Otherwise you won't qualify.

The grant is mandatory (i.e. non-discretionary) where the council is satisfied that renovation, rather than another course of action, is the most appropriate way of bringing a property up to the required standard of fitness for human habitation. Properties falling into this category are liable to include those without bathrooms or indoor toilets, for example. The standard of the property is decided by an inspection by the appropriate council representative.

HOW THE GRANT IS CALCULATED

The amount of grant you will be entitled to will depend on your financial resources. The aim of renovation grants is to provide funding for improvements to those least able to afford them.

The financial test is to enable the council to work out how much they feel you can pay towards the cost of the repairs. If your resources are very low you may be eligible to claim for the total cost of approved renovation work.

The DOE brochure makes the point that if you sell your house within a certain period of time (three years) after receiving the grant then you are required to notify the council. You may then be required to pay back all or part of the grant you received.

You will need to clarify this point when seeking a grant.

HOME IMPROVEMENTS: KEY MONEY MAKING AND SAVING POINTS

1. Generally, look at home improvements for your own benefit. You are only likely to recover a percentage of the costs you incur. Do not over improve.

2. Poor DIY and improvement work can actually diminish the value of your house. Do work to professional standards or not at all.

3. When dealing in a house to improve and sell, buy it at as low a price as you possibly can negotiate.

4. Have a clear idea of what needs to be done to bring the property up to a good standard at which it will sell.

5. Have several quotations from reputable building contractors on the cost of doing the work.

6. If you can obtain a grant be sure you fully understand the procedure and under what terms you may have to pay all or part of it back.

GLOSSARY

ADVANCE:

Money lent, usually by a building society or bank, to enable the borrower to purchase.

BRIDGING LOAN:

A short term loan to complete the purchase of a property while the buyer is waiting for the sale of his home.

COLLATERAL:

Property pledged as a guarantee for the repayment of money.

COMPLETION:

The final legal transfer of ownership of the property.

CONTRACT:

The written legal agreement between the seller and the purchaser with regard to the property.

CONVEYANCER:

Solicitor or licensed conveyancer who arranges the legal aspects of buying and selling property.

CONVEYANCING:

The legal work in the sale and purchase of property.

DEEDS:

Legal document entitling you to a property.

DISBURSEMENTS:

The fees such as stamp duty, Land Registry fees and search fees which are payable to the conveyancer by the purchaser.

EASEMENT:

A landowner's legal right to use the facilities of another's land, for example, a right of way.

EQUITY:

The net value of mortgaged property after the mortgage has been deducted.

EXCHANGE OF CONTRACTS:

The point when both purchaser and seller are legally bound to the transaction and the risk regarding the property passes to the purchaser.

FREEHOLD:

Ownership of the property and the land on which it stands.

GROUND RENT:

Annual charge payable by lease-holders to the freeholder.

HOME BUYERS' SURVEY AND VALUATION:

Surveyor's report on a property – less extensive than a structural survey.

INDEMNITY:

Single payment for an insurance policy to cover the value of the property to lenders when they lend a high percentage of the purchase price.

JOINT TENANCY:

Where two people – for example, husband and wife – hold half shares in a property. If one dies, the survivor takes all.

LAND REGISTRY FEES:

Fees paid by the buyer to register evidence of ownership with the Land Registry. There is a scale of fees set by the government.

LEASE:

Possession of property for the length of time fixed in the lease. This usually includes payment of an annual ground rent.

LEASEHOLD:

Land held under a lease for a fixed number of years.

LESSEE:

The person to whom a lease is granted.

LESSOR:

The person who grants a lease.

MIRAS:

Stands for Mortgage Interest Relief at Source.

MORTGAGE:

A loan made against the security of the property.

MORTGAGOR:

The person borrowing the money.

QUALIFIED VALUER:

A valuer who has passed advanced examinations and is bound by a strict code of professional conduct (look for the letters ARICS, FRICS, ASVA, FSVA).

REDEMPTION:

The final payment on a mortgage. Some building societies make a charge (redemption fee) if a mortgage is ended earlier than was first agreed with them.

REINSTATEMENT VALUE:

The cost of demolishing a house

and rebuilding it including all associated legal and design fees.

STAMP DUTY:

Government tax payable on the purchase of a property with a selling price above a certain level.

SUBJECT TO CONTRACT:

Wording of any agreement before the exchange of contracts which allows either party to withdraw without incurring a penalty.

SURVEY:

Inspection of the property by an independent surveyor normally on behalf of the intending purchaser.

TERM:

The length of time over which the mortgage loan is to be repaid.

VALUATION:

Inspection of the property to ascertain its acceptability to the lender as security against the mortgage loan.

VENDOR:

The person selling the property.

ADDRESSES FOR FURTHER INFORMATION

Society of Licensed Conveyancers, 55 Church Road, Croydon, CR9 1PF (081 681 1001)

Law Society, 50 Chancery Lane, London WC2A 1SX (071 242 1222)

Nationwide Building Society, Nationwide House, Pipers Way, Swindon SN 38 1NW (0793 456374)

Halifax Building Society, Trinity Road, Halifax (0422 333 333)

Royal Institution of Chartered Surveyors, 12 Great George Street, London SW1P 3AD (071 222 7000)

Incorporated Society of Valuers and Auctioneers, 3 Cadogan Gate, London SW1X OAS (071 235 2282)

National Association of Estate Agents, 21 Jury Street, Warwick, CV34 4EH

Building Societies Association/Council of Mortgage Lenders, 3 Savile Row, London W1X IAF (071 437 0655)

National House Building Council, Chiltern Avenue, Amersham, Bucks HP6 5AP (0494 434 477)

British Association of Landscape Industries, Keighley, West Yorkshire BD21 3DR (0535 606139)

Ombudsman for Corporate Estate Agents, P.O. Box 114, Salisbury, Wiltshire SP1 1YQ

Building Societies Ombudsman, Grosvenor Gardens House, 35–37 Grosvenor Gardens, London SW1X 7AW

Federation of Master Builders, 14/15 Great James Street, London WC1N 3DP

Appendix 1

Letters/Correspondence
From Your Estate Agent

XYZ Estates

CONFIRMATION OF INSTRUCTIONS & STANDARD AGENCY TERMS OF ENGAGEMENT IN ACCORDANCE WITH THE NEW *ESTATE AGENCY REGULATIONS*

Between XYZ ESTATES and MR JOHN SMITH

SOLE AGENCY terms for the sale of 10 Nowhere Rd, Anytown

We are pleased to confirm your instructions for the marketing of the above property on your behalf with effect from . . . . to continue thereafter for a minimum period of four months, at an initial asking price of £ . . . .

We will report to you all offers received by XYZ Estates promptly and in the event of a sale being agreed our commission charge will be . . . . . plus VAT at the prevailing rate calculated on the agreed selling price. Such commission will include all advertising expenditure incurred whilst offering the property for sale.

SOLE AGENCY: You will be liable to pay remuneration to us, in addition to any other costs or charges agreed, if at any time unconditional contracts for the sale of your property are exchanged with a purchaser introduced by us during the period of our sole agency or with whom we had negotiations about the property during that period; or with a purchaser introduced by another agent during that period.

SERVICES TO PURCHASER: XYZ Estates will be offering any prospective purchaser financial services in the form of an endowment, or pension related mortgage, or other financial services as may be required and appears appropriate. We may also act in the sale of your purchasers' property for which a fee may be raised, or commission earned, from your purchaser. We may receive a commission should we be successful in providing financial services. There will be no cost to you. This contract is both to inform you that this service will be offered to any prospective purchaser and to confirm your agreement to this contract will be deemed authorisation for offering such services.

Please read the reverse side of this form which further states our terms and conditions.

I/we hereby confirm that as owner/beneficiary/trustee, I/we have read and understood the terms and conditions of this contract.

SIGNED . . . . (Client)

DATE: . . . .

TERMS AND CONDITIONS

(1) Suspension of Marketing
In the event that a prospective purchaser is found for your property and sale letters are sent to the respective solicitors it will be the normal practice of XYZ Estates to cease to actively market your house at that time unless you instruct us otherwise in writing.

(2) Market Advice
Marketing advice is given in the context of the prevailing market conditions. Our advice with regard to the selling price assumes there are no onerous covenants or conditions attached to the property, no structural examination of the property having taken place.

(3) Commission
Commission shall be payable by the client to the Agent plus VAT (at the prevailing rate) when a purchaser has been found for the property and signed a binding contract to purchase the property at the current asking price or such other price as has been agreed by the client after negotiation and subject to other terms and conditions of this contract. This commission shall include all advertising, marketing and out of pocket charges incurred unless otherwise agreed in writing.

(4) Payment of Commission
Payment of commission as in clause (3) and shall apply in respect of any purchasers introduced by the Agents and who may enter into a contract for purchase with the client during the Agency or within six months of the property being withdrawn from the open market with the Agents. Purchasers are deemed to have been introduced to the property by the Agents if they viewed the property during the Agency period or if they have viewed the property after the Agency period but nevertheless were introduced directly or indirectly by the Agents. Indirect instructions include any prospective purchaser who approached the client via the Agents advertisements, sale boards, particulars, or by word of mouth recommendation from anyone who has seen any of these. Payment of charges are due upon invoice. Payment of commission shall become due immediately upon legal completion of the sale. Interest of an annual rate of 3% above Barclays Bank PLCs Base Rate currently in force will occur from the date of account until payment on accounts outstanding more than 28 days.

(5) Negotiations
All negotiations to be carried out through the Agent.

(6) Termination of Instructions
Either party may terminate this contract upon seven days written notice to the other party. The client shall not be entitled to terminate if active negotiations are in progress other than by mutual agreement. In the event of these instructions being terminated or the property withdrawn from sale, commission plus VAT in accordance with Clause (4) hereof may have become due hereunder.

(7) Pre-Contract Deposits
Pre-contract deposits may be taken from prospective purchasers on the understanding that they are 'subject to contract'. In the case of private treaty sales, if deposits are paid they are returnable if the purchaser withdraws prior to entering into a Contract. On exchange of contracts this will be held by the Agents as stakeholder.

(8) Boards
Legislation provides for the erection of one For Sale Board only at the property to be marketed. It is agreed that no additional board, other than XYZ Estates, will be erected at the property. When a prospective purchaser has been introduced to your property and the sale is being progressed by the respective solicitors it will be our normal practice to place a 'sold subject to contract' slip on our sale board, unless otherwise instructed in writing by yourself.

(9) Disclosure of Interest
If XYZ Estates as a Company or one of our staff or a connected person or an associate intend buying a property we are selling, we will make a full and prompt disclosure in writing to the vendor or his solicitor and that member of staff will have nothing further to do with marketing that property. (a) If XYZ Estates are selling a property owned by the Company itself, an employee or connected person, or an associate, we will disclose the relevant facts in writing to the prospective purchaser or his solicitor. If you are aware of any relative working for XYZ Estates you should advise us in writing immediately.

(10) Sales Particulars
The Property Misdescriptions Act 1991 creates a serious offence of making false or misleading statements in the sales particulars or advertising material for a property. In order to avoid making a false or misleading statement it may be necessary for you to provide XYZ Estates with documentary evidence to support claims made within the sales particulars or advertising.

XYZ Estates

Memorandum Of Sale

Subject To Contract

Property:	10, Nowhere Road, Anytown
Vendor:	Mr John Smith
Vendors Address:	10, Nowhere Road, Anytown
Vendors Solicitor:	Sharp and Bent, 6, The High Street, Anytown
Purchaser:	Mr A JONES
Purchaser Address:	268 Green Road, Someplace
Purchasers Solicitor:	Slys, 2, Main Street, Someplace
Purchase Price:	£38,000
Deposit Paid:	None
Mortgage Required:	No mortgage required
Building Society:	Cash purchase
Tenure:	Freehold
Local Authority:	Anytown Borough Council
Fixtures & Fittings:	As per sales particulars
Notes:	We believe the purchaser is not dependent on a sale
Conditions Of Sale:	None
Completion Date:	As soon as possible
Date Sale Agreed:	27th January 19—

XYZ Estates

29th May 199

INVOICE

		VAT
RE: 10 Nowhere Rd., Anytown		
To receipt of your instructions to us to assist in the sale of the above property, to generally offering it on the open market, to preparing illustrated sales particulars, to providing colour photographs, to erecting a sale board (if required), to advertising in the local press, to receiving an offer of £38,000 from Mr A Jones which proved acceptable and to following through to completion.	247.50	52.50
Total	247.50	
VAT	52.50	
Amount due	£300.00	

Please make cheques payable to

Appendix 2

Selling Correspondence
Required From Your Solicitor

Sharp and Bent Solicitors
6 The High St
Anytown

OUR REF:
31st January,

Mr. J. Smith,
10, Nowhere Rd,
Anytown

Dear Mr. Smith

I refer to our telephone conversation today. I write to confirm my estimate of my Firm's charges and your other expenses in connection with your proposed sale and purchase. This estimate will apply in the event that the matter proceeds normally to completion and in the event that you do not proceed with your sale and purchase you will be charged on the basis of time spent and work done up to the point at which you ask me to stop work.

Legal charges on a sale at £38,000.00.	300.00
V.A.T.	52.50
Legal Charges on a purchase at £100,000.00.	360.00
V.A.T.	63.00
Stamp Duty	1,000.00
Land registry fees	230.00
Bank Transfer fee	20.00
Local Search fee	44.00
	£2069.50

I understand that you are not familiar with the City of Bristol and if you find a property in which you are interested and would like to telephone me to discuss it, it may well be that I can give you some information about the area concerned and even possibly the road.

Yours sincerely

Sharp and Bent Solicitors
6 The High Street
Anytown

YOUR REF.	OUR REF.	When calling, please ask for: Miss Small
		VAT Registration No.

To Legal Costs	COSTS	
Sale of 10, Nowhere Road, Anytown		
TO our Professional Charges in connection with taking your instructions; obtaining Title Deeds; writing Purchasers' Solicitors; drafting Contract; applying for Office Copy Entries/preparing Epitome of Title; submitting draft Contract and Title to Purchasers' Solicitors; replying to Enquiries before Contract: obtaining your signature to the Contract; exchanging Contracts; obtaining draft Transfer for approval; replying to Requisitions on Title; obtaining your execution to the Transfer; requesting Estate Agents' Account and obtaining your approval of same; completing; settling with Estate Agents; submitting Title Deeds to Purchasers' Solicitors.	300	00

Date of Exchange of Contracts	5th May 199
Date of Completion	21st May 199

VAT @17.5% — 52 | 50

DISBURSEMENTS

TOTAL COSTS, DISBURSEMENTS AND VAT £ 352 | 50

Appendix 3

Information Sellers Provide Prospective Purchasers

The following forms are part of the Law Society's TransAction scheme. As a seller you will have to provide much of this information to your purchaser even if you do not use TransAction.

SELLER'S PROPERTY INFORMATION FORM

Address of the Property: _____

_____

_____

IMPORTANT NOTE TO SELLERS

* Please complete this form carefully. It will be sent to the buyer's solicitor and may be seen by the buyer. If you are unsure how to answer any of the questions, ask your solicitor before doing so.

* For many of the questions you need only tick the correct answer. Where necessary, please give more detailed answers on a separate sheet of paper. Then send all the replies to your solicitor so that the information can be passed to the buyer's solicitor.

* The answers should be those of the person whose name is on the deeds. If there is more than one of you, you should prepare the answers together.

* It is very important that your answers are correct because the buyer will rely on them in deciding whether to go ahead. Incorrect information given to the buyer through your solicitor, or mentioned to the buyer in conversation between you, may mean that the buyer can claim compensation from you or even refuse to complete the purchase.

* It does not matter if you do not know the answer to any question so long as you say so.

* The buyer will be told by his solicitor that he takes the property as it is. If he wants more information about it, he should get it from his own advisers, not from you.

* If anything changes after you fill in this questionnaire but before the sale is completed, tell your solicitor immediately. This is as important as giving the right answers in the first place.

* Please pass to your solicitor immediately any notices you have received which affect the property. The same goes for notices which arrive at any time before completion.

* If you have a tenant, tell your solicitor immediately there is any change in the arrangements but do nothing without asking your solicitor first.

* You should let your solicitor have any letters, agreements or other documents which help answer the questions. If you know of any which you are not supplying with these anwers, please tell your solicitor about them.

* Please complete and return the separate Fixtures, Fittings and Contents Form. It is an important document which will form part of the contract between you and the buyer. Unless you mark clearly on it the items which you wish to remove, they will be included in the sale and you will not be able to take them with you when you move.

Part I – to be completed by the seller

1   Boundaries

"Boundaries" mean any fence, wall, hedge or ditch which marks the edge of your property.

1.1 Looking towards the house from the road, who either owns or accepts responsibility for the boundary:

Please tick the right answer

(a) on the left?

WE DO	NEXT DOOR	SHARED	NOT KNOWN

(b) on the right?

WE DO	NEXT DOOR	SHARED	NOT KNOWN

(c) at the back?

WE DO	NEXT DOOR	SHARED	NOT KNOWN

1.2 If you have answered "not known", which boundaries have you actually repaired or maintained?

(Please give details) _____

_____

_____

1.3 Do you know of any boundary being moved in the last 20 years?

(Please give details) _____

_____

_____

2   Disputes

2.1 Do you know of any disputes about this or any neighbouring property?

NO	YES: (PLEASE GIVE DETAILS)

_____

_____

_____

2.2 Have you received any complaints about anything you have, or have not, done as owners?

NO	YES: (PLEASE GIVE DETAILS)

_____

_____

Prop 1/2

Please tick the right answer

2.3 Have you made any such complaints to any neighbour about what the neighbour has or has not done?

NO	YES: (PLEASE GIVE DETAILS)

3   Notices

3.1 Have you either sent or received any letters or notices which affect your property or the neighbouring property in any way (for example, from or to neighbours, the council or a government department)?

NO	YES	COPY ENCLOSED	TO FOLLOW	LOST

3.2 Have you had any negotiations or discussions with any neighbour or any local or other authority which affect the property in any way?

NO	YES: (PLEASE GIVE DETAILS)

4   Guarantees

4.1 Are there any guarantees or insurance policies of the following types:

(a) NHBC Foundation 15 or Newbuild?

NO	YES	COPIES ENCLOSED	WITH DEEDS	LOST

(b) Damp course?

NO	YES	COPIES ENCLOSED	WITH DEEDS	LOST

(c) Double glazing?

NO	YES	COPIES ENCLOSED	WITH DEEDS	LOST

(d) Electrical work?

NO	YES	COPIES ENCLOSED	WITH DEEDS	LOST

(e) Roofing?

NO	YES	COPIES ENCLOSED	WITH DEEDS	LOST

(f) Rot or infestation?

NO	YES	COPIES ENCLOSED	WITH DEEDS	LOST

(g) Central heating?

NO	YES	COPIES ENCLOSED	WITH DEEDS	LOST

(h) Anything similar? (e.g. cavity wall insulation)

NO	YES	COPIES ENCLOSED	WITH DEEDS	LOST

(i) Do you have written details or the work done to obtain any of these guarantees?

NO	YES	COPIES ENCLOSED	WITH DEEDS	LOST

Prop 1/3

Please tick the right answer

4.2 Have you made or considered making claims under
any of these?

NO	YES: (PLEASE GIVE DETAILS)

---

5   Services

(This section applies to gas, electrical and water
supplies, sewerage disposal and telephone cables.)

5.1 Please tick which services are connected to the
property.

GAS	ELEC.	WATER	DRAINS	TEL.	CABLE T.V.

5.2 Do any drains, pipes or wires for these cross any
neighbour's property?

NOT KNOWN	YES: (PLEASE GIVE DETAILS)

5.3 Do any drains, pipes or wires leading to any
neighbour's property cross your property?

NOT KNOWN	YES: (PLEASE GIVE DETAILS)

5.4 Are you aware of any agreement which is not with
the deeds about any of these services?

NOT KNOWN	YES: (PLEASE GIVE DETAILS)

---

6   Sharing with the neighbours

6.1 Are you aware of any responsibility to contribute
to the cost of anything used jointly, such as the repair
of a shared drive, boundary or drain?

YES: (PLEASE GIVE DETAILS)	NO

Please tick the right answer

6.2 Do you contribute to the cost of repair of anything used by the neighbourhood, such as the maintenance of a private road?

YES	NO

6.3 If so, who is responsible for organising the work and collecting the contributions?

_____

6.4 Please give details of all such sums paid or owing, and explain if they are paid on a regular basis or only as and when work is required.

_____

_____

6.5 Do you need to go next door if you have to repair or decorate your building or maintain any of the boundaries?

YES	NO

6.6 If "Yes", have you always been able to do so without objection by the neighbours?

YES	NO: please give details of any objection under the answer to question 2 (disputes)

6.7 Do any of your neighbours need to come onto your land to repair or decorate their building or maintain the boundaries?

YES	NO

6.8 If so, have you ever objected?

NO	YES: please give details of any objection under the answer to question 2 (disputes)

7 | Arrangements and rights

Are there any other formal or informal arrangements which give someone else rights over your property?

NO	YES: (PLEASE GIVE DETAILS)

_____

_____

8 | Occupiers

8.1 Does anyone other than you live in the property?
If "No" go to question 9.1.
If "Yes" please give their full names and (if under 18) their ages

YES	NO

_____

_____

Prop 1/5

Please tick the right answer

8.2(a)(i) Do any of them have any right to stay on the property with your permission?

(These rights may have arisen without you realising, e.g. if they have paid towards the cost of buying the house, paid for improvements or helped you make your mortgage payments)

NO:	YES: (PLEASE GIVE DETAILS)

8.2(a)(ii) Are any of them tenants or lodgers?

NO	YES: (PLEASE GIVE DETAILS AND A COPY OF ANY TENANCY AGREEMENT)

8.2(b) Have they all agreed to sign the contract for sale agreeing to leave with you (or earlier)?

NO	YES: (PLEASE GIVE DETAILS)

9 Restrictions

If you have changed the use of the property of carried out any building work on it, please read the note below and answer these questions. If you have not, please go on to Question 10.

Note The title deeds of some properties include clauses which are called "restrictive covenants". For example, these may forbid the owner of the house to carry out any building work or to use it for the purpose of a business – unless someone else (often the builder of the house) gives his consent.

9.1(a) Do you know of any "restrictive covenant" which applies to your house or land?

NO	YES

(b) If "Yes", did you ask for consent for the work or change of use?

NO	YES: (PLEASE GIVE DETAILS AND A COPY OF ANY CONSENT)

9.2 If consent was needed but not obtained, please explain why not.

9.3 If the reply to 9.1(a) is "Yes", please give the name
and address of the person from whom consent has to
be obtained.

_____

_____

10   Planning

Please tick the right answer

10.1 Is the property used only as a private home?

YES	NO: (PLEASE GIVE DETAILS)

_____

10.2(a) Is the property a listed building or in a
conservation area?

YES	NO	NOT KNOWN

(b) If "Yes", what work has been carried out since
it was listed or the area became a conservation area?

_____

10.3(a) Has there been any building work on the
property in the last four years?

NO	YES: (PLEASE GIVE DETAILS)

(b) If "Yes", was planning permission, building
regulation approval or listed building consent obtained?

NO	NOT REQUIRED	YES:	COPIES ENCLOSED	TO FOLLOW	LOST

10.4 Have you applied for planning permission,
building regulation approval or listed building consent
at any time?

NO	YES:	COPIES ENCLOSED	TO FOLLOW	LOST

10.5 If "Yes", has any of the work been carried
out?

NO	YES: (PLEASE GIVE DETAILS)

10.6(a) Has there been any change of use of the
property in the last ten years? (e.g dividing into flats,
combining flats or using part for business use)?

NO	YES: (PLEASE GIVE DETAILS)

(b) If "Yes", was planning permission obtained?

NO	NOT REQUIRED	YES:	COPIES ENCLOSED	TO FOLLOW	LOST

11 | Fixtures

Please tick the right answer

11.1 If you have sold through an estate agent, are all items listed in its particulars included in the sale?

YES	NO

If "No" you should instruct the estate agent to write to everyone concerned correcting this error.

11.2 Do you own outright everything included in the sale?

YES	NO: (PLEASE GIVE DETAILS)

(*You must give details of anything which may not be yours to sell, for example, anything rented or on H.P.*)

---

12 | Expenses

Have you ever had to pay for the use of the property?

NO	YES: (PLEASE GIVE DETAILS)

(*Ignore rates, water rates, community charge and gas, electricity and phone bills. Disclose anything else: examples are the clearance of cess pool or septic tank, drainage rate, rent charge.*)

---

13 | General

Is there any other information which you think the buyer may have a right to know?

NO	YES: (PLEASE GIVE DETAILS)

Signature(s) . . . .

. . . .

Date . . . .

THE LAW SOCIETY

This form is part of The Law Society's TransAction scheme. © The Law Society 1994
The Law Society is the professional body for solicitors in England and Wales
March 1994

SELLER'S PROPERTY INFORMATION FORM

Part II — to be completed by the seller's solicitor and to be sent with Part I

Address of the Property:

_____

_____

_____

SPECIMEN

A   Boundaries

Does the information in the deeds agree with the seller's reply to 1.1 in Part I?

Please tick the right answer

YES	NO (PLEASE GIVE DETAILS)

_____

_____

B   Relevant documents

Are you aware of any correspondence, notices, consents or other documents other than those disclosed in Questions 3 or 4 of Part I?

YES	NO

_____

_____

C   Guarantees

If appropriate, have guarantees been assigned to the seller and notice of an assignment given?

YES	NO	NOT KNOWN

If "Yes", please supply copies, including copies of all guarantees not enclosed with Part I of this Form

D   Services

Please give full details of all legal rights enjoyed to ensure the benefit of uninterrupted services, e.g. easements, wayleaves, licences, etc.

_____

_____

Prop 2/1

E   Adverse Interests

Please give full details of all overriding interests
affecting the property as defined by the Land
Registration Act 1925, s.70(1).

F   Restrictions

Who has the benefit of any restrictive covenants? If
known, please provide the name and address of the
person or company having such benefit or the name and
address of his or its solicitors.

G   Mechanics of Sale

Please tick the right answer

(a) Is this sale dependent on the seller buying another
property?

YES	NO

(b) If "Yes", what stage have the negotiations
reached?

(c) Does the seller require a mortgage?

YES	NO

(d) If "Yes", has an offer been received and/or
accepted or a mortgage certificate obtained?

YES	NO

H   Deposit

Will the whole or part of the deposit be used on a
related transaction?

If so, please state to whom it will be paid and in what
capacity it will be held by them.

NO	YES: (PLEASE GIVE DETAILS)

Seller's Solicitor ....

Date ....

Reminder
1. The Fixtures, Fittings and Contents Form should be supplied in addition to the information above.
2. Copies of all planning permissions, buildings regulations consents, guarantees, assignments and notices should be
supplied with this form.
3. If the property is leasehold, also complete the Seller's Leasehold Information Form.

THE LAW SOCIETY

SELLER'S LEASEHOLD INFORMATION FORM

Address of the Property:

_____

_____

_____

If you live in leasehold property, please answer the following questions. Some people live in blocks of flats, others in large houses converted into flats and others in single leasehold houses. These questions cover all types of leasehold property, but some of them may not apply to your property. In that case please answer them N/A.

The instructions set out at the front of the Seller's Property Information Form apply to this form as well. Please read them again before giving your answers to these questions.

If you are unsure how to answer any of the questions, ask your solicitor.

Part I – to be completed by the seller

1 Management Company

1.1 If there is a management company which is run by the tenants please supply any of the following documents which are in your possession:

Please mark the appropriate box

(a) Memorandum and articles of association of the company.

ENCLOSED	TO FOLLOW	LOST	N/A

(b) Your share or membership certificate.

ENCLOSED	TO FOLLOW	LOST	N/A

(c) The management accounts for the last 3 years.

ENCLOSED	TO FOLLOW	LOST	N/A

(d) Copy of any regulations made by either the landlord or the company additional to the rules contained in the lease.

ENCLOSED	TO FOLLOW	LOST	N/A

(e) The names and addresses of the secretary and treasurer of the company.

_____

_____

_____

Prop 4/1

2   The Landlord

2.1 What is the name and address of your landlord?

_____

_____

_____

2.2 If the landlord employs an agent to collect the rent. what is the name and address of that agent?

_____

_____

_____

2.3 Do you have the landlord's receipt for the last rent payment?

YES

(Please tick box and send it with these answers)

NO: (Explain why not)

_____

_____

2.4 Do you pay a share of the maintenance costs of the building?

YES

(Please tick box and send the receipt. or demand, for the last payment with these answers)

NO: (Explain why not)

_____

_____

3   Maintenance Charges

3.1 Do you know of any unusual expense likely to show in the maintenance charge accounts in the next year or two?

Please mark the appropriate box

YES	NO

If "Yes", please give details.

_____

_____

_____

3.2   How much have you paid for maintenance charges in each of the last 3 years?

_____

3.3   Do you have the receipts for these?

NO	YES	ENCLOSED	TO FOLLOW	LOST

3.4 Do you know of any problems in the last 3 years between flat owners and the landlord or maintenance company about maintenance charges, or the method of management?

YES	NO

If "Yes", please give details.

_____

3.5 Have you challenged the maintenance charge or any expense in the last 3 years?

YES	NO

If "Yes", please give details.

_____

3.6 Do you know if the landlord has had any problems in collecting the maintenance charges from other flat owners?

YES	NO

If "Yes", please give details.

_____

4   Notices

A landlord may serve a notice on a printed form or in the form of a letter and your buyer will wish to know if anything of this sort has been received.

4.1 Have you had a notice from the landlord that he wants to sell his interest in the building?

NO	YES	COPY ENCLOSED	TO FOLLOW	LOST

4.2 Have you had any other notice or letter about the building, its use, its condition or its repair and maintenance?

NO	YES	COPY ENCLOSED	TO FOLLOW	LOST

5   Consents

Are you aware of any charges in the terms of the lease or of the landlord giving any consents under the lease? (This may be in a deed, a letter or even verbal) If not in writing, please supply details.

NO	NOT KNOWN	YES:	COPIES ENCLOSED	TO FOLLOW	LOST

6   Complaints

6.1 Have you received any complaints from the landlord, any landlord above him, management company or any other tenant about anything you have or have not done?

YES	NO

If "Yes", please give details.

_____

Please mark the appropriate box

6.2 Have you had cause for complaint to any of them?

YES	NO

If "Yes", please give details.

_____

_____

_____

6.3 Have you complained to anyone else about the conduct of any other occupier?

YES	NO

If "Yes", please give details.

_____

_____

_____

7 | Insurance

7.1 Do you have to arrange the insurance on the building?

YES	NO

If "No", go to Question 7.4

7.2 If "Yes", do you have a copy of the insurance policy?

COPY ENCLOSED	TO FOLLOW	LOST

7.3 Do you have a copy of the receipt for the last payment of the premium?

COPY ENCLOSED	TO FOLLOW	LOST

7.4 Do you have a copy of the insurance policy arranged by the landlord or the management company and a copy of the schedule for the current year?

NO	YES	COPIES ENCLOSED	TO FOLLOW	LOST

8 | Decoration

8.1 If outside decoration is your responsibility, when was it last done?

IN THE YEAR 19	NOT KNOWN

Prop 4/4

Please mark the appropriate box

9.1 Are you aware of any alterations having been made to your property since the lease was orginally granted?

YES	NO	NOT KNOWN

If "Yes", please supply details.

_____

_____

9.2 If "Yes", was landlord's consent obtained?

NO	NOT KNOWN	NOT REQUIRED	YES:	COPIES ENCLOSED	TO FOLLOW	LOST

10 Occupation

10.1 Are you now occupying the property as your sole or main home?

YES	NO

10.2 Have you occupied the property as your sole or main home (apart from usual holidays and business trips) –

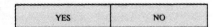

(a) continuously throughout the last twelve months?

YES	NO

(b) continuously throughout the last three years?

YES	NO

(c) for periods totalling at least three years during the last ten years?

YES	NO

11 Enfranchisement

11.1 Have you served on your immediate or superior landlord a formal notice under the enfranchisement legislation stating your desire to buy the freehold or be granted an extended lease?

NO	YES	COPY ENCLOSED	COPY TO FOLLOW	COPY LOST

If so, please supply a copy.

11.2 If the property is a flat in a block, have you served on the immediate or any superior landlord any formal notices under the enfranchisement legislation relating to the possible collective purchase of the freehold of the block or part of it?
If so, please supply a copy.

NO	YES	COPY ENCLOSED	COPY TO FOLLOW	COPY LOST

11.3 Has any letter or notice been served upon you in response?

NO	YES	COPY ENCLOSED	COPY TO FOLLOW	COPY LOST

Signature(s): ....

....

Date: ....

SELLER'S LEASEHOLD INFORMATION FORM

Part II – to be completed by the seller's solicitor and to be sent with Part I

Address of the Property:

A   Documents and Information

(1) In respect of any items not enclosed with Part I of this form, please supply copies or confirm that copies will be supplied in due course.

Please mark the appropriate box

	ENCLOSED	TO FOLLOW	N/A
1.1(a) Memo and arts			
1.1(b) Share cert			
1.1(c) Accounts			
1.1(d) Regulations			
2.3 Rent receipt			

	ENCLOSED	TO FOLLOW	N/A
3.3 Receipt for service charge			
4.2 Notices			
6.2 Seller's insurance			
6.3 Seller's premium receipt			
6.4 Landlord's insurance			

(2) If apparent from the papers in your possession, please provide details of any names and addresses or other information that the seller was unable to provide on Part I of this form. Please state if any of that information will be supplied at a later date.

B   Landlord (including Management Company)

(1) Please provide name and address of the recipient of notice of assignment and charge.

(2) Do the insurers make a practice of recording the interest of the buyer's mortgagee and the buyer on the policy?

Please mark the appropriate box

YES	NO	NOT KNOWN

(3) Please supply a copy of the fire certificate.

SUPPLIED	TO FOLLOW	N/A

(4) How many flats are there in the building?

(5) Are all of them let on identical leases? If not, in what respect do they differ?

YES	NO	NOT KNOWN

Prop 5/1

(6) Has the landlord experienced problems with the collection of maintenance charges as they fall due? If so, please supply details.

Pleae mark the appropriate box

YES	NO	NOT KNOWN

C   Notices

(1) In respect of any items or information not enclosed with Part I of this form, please answer the following questions:

1(1) Please supply details of any notices served upon the seller under the Landlord and Tenant Act 1987 indicating that the landlord is proposing to sell the landlord's reversionary interest in the building.

ENCLOSED	TO FOLLOW	N/A

1(2) Please state what is the present position as a result of the service of the notice.

_____

_____

2(1) Please supply a copy of any Notice served by the seller under the Leasehold Reform Act 1967 or the Leasehold Housing and Urban Development Act 1993.

ENCLOSED	TO FOLLOW	N/A

2(2) Please supply a copy of any letter or Notice served upon the seller in response.

ENCLOSED	TO FOLLOW	N/A

3(1) Please supply details of any notices served under Sections 18–30 Landlord and Tenant Act 1985.

_____

_____

3(2) Has the seller paid all contributions required by the notice?

YES	NO

If not, please state reasons.

_____

_____

D   House Conversions

If planning consent cannot be produced, please provide a copy of an established use certificate.
In the absence of either, please supply evidence of permitted use.

ENCLOSED	TO FOLLOW	N/A

_____

_____

Reminder

Copies of any relevant documents should be supplied with this Form.

Seller's Solicitor ....

Date ....

THE LAW SOCIETY

Prop 5/2

FIXTURES FITTINGS AND CONTENTS (2ND EDITION)

Address of the Property:

1. Place a tick in one of these three columns against every item.

2. The second column ("excluded from the sale") is for items on the list which you are proposing to take with you when you move. If you are prepared to sell any of these to the buyer, please write the price you wish to be paid beside the name of the item and the buyer can then decide whether or not to accept your offer to sell.

	INCLUDED IN THE SALE	EXCLUDED FROM THE SALE	NONE AT THE PROPERTY
TV Aerial/Satellite Dish			
Radio Aerial			
Immersion Heater			
Hot Water Cylinder Jacket			
Roof Insulation			
Wall Heaters			
Night Storage Heater			
Gas/Electric Fires			
Light Fittings:			
Ceiling Lights	☐	☐	☐
Wall Lights	☐	☐	☐
Lamp Shades	☐	☐	☐
N.B. If these are to be removed, it is assumed that they will be replaced by ceiling rose and socket, flex, bulb holder and bulb.			
Switches			
Electric Points			
Dimmer Switches			

SPECIMEN

This form comprises 6 pages. Please ensure you complete all sections on all pages. Please turn over to next page. PROP6/1

	INCLUDED IN THE SALE	EXCLUDED FROM THE SALE	NONE AT THE PROPERTY
Fluorescent Lighting			
Outside Lights			
Telephone Receivers:			
British Telecom	☐	☐	☐
Own	☐	☐	☐
Burglar Alarm System			
Complete Central Heating System			
Extractor Fans			
Doorbell/Chimes			
Door Knocker			
Door Furniture:			
Internal	☐	☐	☐
External	☐	☐	☐
Double Glazing			
Window Fitments			
Shutters/Grills			
Curtain Rails			
Curtain Poles			
Pelmets			
Venetian Blinds			
Roller Blinds			
Curtains (Including Net Curtains):			
Lounge	☐	☐	☐
Dining Room	☐	☐	☐

SPECIMEN

	INCLUDED IN THE SALE	EXCLUDED FROM THE SALE	NONE AT THE PROPERTY
Kitchen	☐	☐	☐
Bathroom	☐	☐	☐
Bedroom 1	☐	☐	☐
Bedroom 2	☐	☐	☐
Bedroom 3	☐	☐	☐
Bedroom 4	☐	☐	☐
Other Rooms (state which)			
1	☐	☐	☐
2	☐	☐	☐
3	☐	☐	☐
Carpets and other Floor Covering:			
Lounge	☐	☐	☐
Dining Room	☐	☐	☐
Kitchen	☐	☐	☐
Hall, Stairs and Landing	☐	☐	☐
Bathroom	☐	☐	☐
Bedroom 1	☐	☐	☐
Bedroom 2	☐	☐	☐
Bedroom 3	☐	☐	☐
Bedroom 4			
Other Rooms (state which)			
1	☐	☐	☐

	INCLUDED IN THE SALE	EXCLUDED FROM THE SALE	NONE AT THE PROPERTY
2	☐	☐	☐
3	☐	☐	☐
Storage Units in Kitchen			
Kitchen Fitments:			
Fitted Cupboards and Shelves	☐	☐	☐
Refrigerator/ Fridge-Freezer	☐	☐	☐
Oven	☐	☐	☐
Extractor Hood	☐	☐	☐
Hob	☐	☐	☐
Cutlery Rack	☐	☐	☐
Spice Rack	☐	☐	☐
Other (state which)			
1	☐	☐	☐
2	☐	☐	☐
3	☐	☐	☐
Kitchen Furniture:			
Washing Machine	☐	☐	☐
Dishwasher	☐	☐	☐
Tumble-Drier	☐	☐	☐
Cooker	☐	☐	☐
Other (state which)			
1	☐	☐	☐

	INCLUDED IN THE SALE	EXCLUDED FROM THE SALE	NONE AT THE PROPERTY
2	☐	☐	☐
3	☐	☐	☐
Bathroom Fitments:			
Cabinet	☐	☐	☐
Towel Rails	☐	☐	☐
Soap and Tooth-brush Holders	☐	☐	☐
Toilet Roll Holders	☐	☐	☐
Fitted Shelves/Cupboards	☐	☐	☐
Other Sanitary Fittings	☐	☐	☐
Shower			
Shower Fittings			
Shower Curtain			
Bedroom Fittings:			
Shelves	☐	☐	☐
Fitted Wardrobes	☐	☐	☐
Fitted Cupboards			
Fitted Shelving/Cupboards			
Fitted Units			
Wall Mirrors			
Picture Hooks			
Plant Holders			
Clothes Line			
Rotary Line			

SPECIMEN

	INCLUDED IN THE SALE	EXCLUDED FROM THE SALE	NONE AT THE PROPERTY
Garden Shed			
Greenhouse			
Garden Ornaments			
Trees, Plants and Shrubs			
Garden Produce			
Stock of Oil/Solid Fuel/Propane Gas			
Water Butts			
Dustbins			
Other			

Signed Seller(s)
....

....

THE LAW SOCIETY

This form is part of The Law Society's TransAction scheme. © The Law Society 1992.
The Law Society is the professional body for solicitors in England and Wales.
January 1994